More
Hypnotic Inductions

Also by George Gafner

Clinical Applications of Hypnosis
Hypnotic Techniques, with Sonja Benson
Handbook of Hypnotic Inductions, with Sonja Benson

A NORTON PROFESSIONAL BOOK

More
Hypnotic Inductions

GEORGE GAFNER

W.W. Norton & Company
New York • London

For information about permission to reproduce
selections from this book, write to
Permissions, W. W. Norton & Company, Inc.,
500 Fifth Avenue, New York, NY 10110

Manufacturing by Quebecor World-Fairfield Press
Book design by Ken Gross
Production Manger: Leeann Graham

Library of Congress Cataloging-in-Publication Data

Gafner, George, 1947–
   More hypnotic inductions / George Gafner.
      p.   cm.
   Includes bibliographical references and index.
   ISBN 13: 978-0-393-70518-8
   ISBN 10: 0-393-70518-8
   Hypnotism—Therapeutic use. I. Title.

RC495.G274 2006
615.8'512—dc22   2006048273

ISBN 13: 978-0-393-70518-8
ISBN 10: 0-393-70518-8

W. W. Norton & Company, Inc., 500 Fifth Avenue, New York, N.Y. 10110
www.wwnorton.com
W. W. Norton & Company Ltd., Castle House, 75/76 Wells St., London W1T 3QT

1 2 3 4 5 6 7 8 9 0

Contents

Acknowledgments

I want to thank those who have contributed material, read the manuscript, or otherwise provided support for this manuscript. Those include my wife, Judy, for her ongoing love and understanding; Deborah Malmud and her staff at Norton Professional Books; and Patricia Haynes, Dorothy Stoops, Alice Packard, Dave Emelity, Ingrid Jacobs, Kami Sandhu, Chanel Helgason, Michael Wm. Marks, Matt Weyer, Chuck Mutter, Sonja Benson, Lynn Flance, Larry Aronow, Allison Davis, Melissa Sisco, Heidi Summers, Bob Camwell, and Karen Douglas. Without your generous assistance this book would not have been possible.

Introduction

You're on a boat, perhaps a cruise ship, heading out to an island where you'll spend your vacation at a resort. The island is your final destination, but you have to get there first.

"Getting there" is one way to think of the hypnotic induction, and your vacation comprises the therapy component of hypnosis, or what you do with your clients after helping them achieve trance.

Maybe your idea of a vacation is backpacking in the woods, or spending a week in the city. Whatever it is, you have to *get there first*, and that's what this book is about—the induction phase of hypnosis. In my first book on this topic (with Sonja Benson), *Handbook of Hypnotic Inductions* (2000), a variety of inductions and deepenings were covered, and Sonja and I have been immensely pleased by its reception in many countries. At conferences, practitioners time and time again have told us how pleased they are to be able to select from a number of inductions that they can apply to a host of client situations.

Since publication of the *Handbook*, I have continued to develop new inductions and experiment with new material, occasionally becoming intrigued by something I see or hear, and then a story begins to take shape. My previous book had little material specifically for sleep, but I've written sleep inductions in this book in response to many clients being referred for insomnia. In short, you'll find a bounty of inductions here.

If therapists need, for example, a confusional induction, or an induction for children, they can just pick up the book and read about it. Now, *reading* it may be a problem for some practitioners. Why? Because many of us were taught that instead of relying on a script, we should be able to spontaneously generate the right words while pacing and leading the client's ongoing response. After all, if you watch one of the masters, like Michael Yapko or Jeff Zeig, that's how they do it. They never have to glance down at a 3" x 5" card, much less read from something that is several pages long.

I don't need to read from a script either—most of the time. However, sometimes, as in the case of a complicated, precisely worded induction, I choose to read it because I simply can't remember the whole thing. Inductions aside, if the therapy component of hypnosis itself calls for one or more anecdotes or stories, there again I often read them in order to make sure I get them right. My clients come to expect that I'll read to them. In doing hypnosis for 25 years I've never yet had a client say, "George, I think you'd be more effective if you were spontaneous instead of reading to me."

Reading from a script is commonplace in many programs that teach hypnosis. Matt Weyer, a clinical psychologist at the Carl T. Hayden Veterans Affairs Health Care System in Phoenix, has interns learn the process by inducing trance on each other before doing hypnosis with clients. They begin by reading inductions and stories in the training group, and later, when treating the anxiety disorders and chronic pain of their clients, the interns continue to read the same material. Matt encourages interns to practice without relying on a script. Some do and some don't.

The same holds true in my own hypnosis training program in Tucson, where I train fourth-year residents in psychiatry, psychology interns and externs, and various master-level interns. For years I conducted this program with clinical psychologist Bob Hall until his unfortunate death in 2005. When students clung to their scripts he would remind them, "Okay, time to take off the training wheels." Some become adept at improvising and are soon riding a unicycle, while others, after years of private practice, wear the rubber off and are riding on the rims, steadfastly sticking to their training wheels. And that's fine, it's no big deal!

This book is designed to be a major tool in your toolbox. These inductions and deepenings have been tested on clients with tough problems—chronic pain, PTSD, insomnia, and various other disorders. Although this material is primarily intended for adults, I have included a section on hypnosis with children and adolescents, as younger clients are also a part of my practice.

It was a pleasure to write this book. I hope it brings you many happy inductions.

More
Hypnotic Inductions

1

Preliminary Considerations

WHAT IS HYPNOSIS?

In 2005 the American Psychological Association (APA) adopted a definition of hypnosis: "Hypnosis typically involves an introduction to the procedure during which the subject is told that suggestions for imaginative experiences will be presented" (Green, Barabasz, Barrett, & Montgomery, 2005, p. 104). This definition goes on to narrowly limit, and unfortunately, obfuscate instead of clarify. Some have criticized this as no definition at all, but rather a description of various facets of hypnotic experience and related issues, something that ignores naturally occuring hypnotic states outside the office, and reinforces the negative stereotype of the client as a passive recipient (Yapko, 2005–2006).

Clients new to hypnosis need clarity and directness. That's why I continue to give them the APA's 1993 definition of hypnosis: "A procedure wherein changes in sensations, perceptions, thoughts, feelings, or behavior are suggested." I may also tell clients that hypnosis has been called believed-in imagination, controlled dissociation, guided daydreaming, a halfway point between sleep and consciousness, a narrowing of conscious attention, and facilitation of unconscious receptivity. I want to briefly connect with clients about the definition, answer any questions they may have, and move on to helping them with their particular problem.

So, could definitions of hypnosis also apply to meditation, guided imagery, stress management, or myriad other techniques? Quite possibly: *Guided imagery* and *meditation* are positive terms, whereas for some people, *hypnosis* carries a negative connotation. Therein lie the two aspects of the hypnosis coin: the perception of "mind control" on one side, and power and mystery on the other. You can't have one without the other. Progressive muscle relaxation (PMR), a procedure to relax the body, is not hypnosis, but if you add *imagery* to PMR, it starts to look like hypnosis even though it isn't called hypnosis.

We should never forget the baggage attached to hypnosis in the public mind. I've had many clients who say things like, "Give me any kind of relaxation or guided imagery you want, but *don't* give me hypnosis." With those people I usually do an imaginal PMR (e.g., "a warm liquid covering your body") or one of the directive/guided imagery inductions in this book, gain their trust, talk some more, and then they're usually ready to accept "hypnosis." If they're still reluctant, I suggest they seek help elsewhere.

In introducing clients to trancework, I always ask them about naturally occurring trance states: "Tell me about when you're absorbed in something pleasant, perhaps listening to music, or driving your car, when you lose track of time. . . . " I let them know that hypnosis in the office is essentially the same process, "and with a guide, people invariably go deeper."

If you employ an induction in this book with your clients, you can call it relaxation or guided imagery if you want, but I would call it hypnosis. A general rule of thumb: If you call it hypnosis, it is hypnosis.

NEUROIMAGING STUDIES AND HYPNOSIS

With functional magnetic resonance imaging (fMRI) scientists for the first time can view what is going on in the brain during hypnotic suggestion. In one study, when hypnotized subjects were asked to *see* colors, the color-processing parts of their brains lit up, despite the absence of any real color in front of them. In another fMRI study, when hypnotized subjects were asked to *see* certain patterns in color, the participants showed activation in the same area of the brain—the right fusiform gyrus—as when they viewed actual color prints (Winerman, 2006).

Another experiment found that hypnotically induced pain activated the same brain areas as "real" pain. Researchers learned that the same pain-processing areas of the brain—in the thalamus, anterior cingulate cortex, and other areas—were as active as in subjects who actually touched a 120-degree metal probe. Meanwhile, subjects who simply imagined the pain did not show the same active brain areas.

This new research may soon explain why some people are more hypnotizable than others, and also provide insight into who is most likely to benefit from hypnosis (Winerman, 2006).

WHO SHOULD PRACTICE HYPNOSIS?

"Hypnotists" advertise everywhere and almost anyone can learn online or in brief training to be a hypnotist. They can hypnotize you into losing weight, quitting smoking, not being depressed, and cure you of virtually any malady. You don't need a state license to call yourself a hypnotist, nor are you accountable to a professional society and its code of ethics. I belabor the point because this phenomenon, like stage hypnosis, is part of the public's perception of hypnosis, and you may have to address it with your clients. It is worth pointing out that hypnosis is used in many legitimate ways; for example, by police departments to help victims remember details from a crime, and by some dental hygienists and dentists as well as emergency medical personnel for acute pain.

What I am addressing in this book is *clinical hypnosis*, something done as part of psychotherapy, and as such, hypnosis should be practiced by licensed master's level and above mental health practitioners, such as psychologists, psychiatrists, social workers, psychiatric nurses, counselors, and others who have received training in hypnosis from an organization such as the Milton H. Erickson Foundation, or one of its component societies, or the American Society of Clinical Hypnosis (ASCH), or equivalent societies in the United States and abroad.

Chuck Mutter, M.D., training director for ASCH, provided this litmus test for an organization that offers training in hypnosis in the United States: "Ask them if they are endorsed by either the Society of Clinical and Experimental Hypnosis or ASCH" (Mutter, personal communication, 2003). If the answer is no, look elsewhere.

I have known many lay hypnotists, some of them well read and highly skilled. They are proud to be called hypnotists, just as some highly regarded mental health professionals call themselves hypnotists. I hate being called a hypnotist, and hypnotherapist is only a bit better. Both terms imply that all you do is hypnosis. If I have acute grief and need to talk I probably won't be calling on either a hypnotist or a hypnotherapist. I consider myself a therapist who practices hypnosis among other modalities. Hypnosis is a major interest of mine, but the reality is that I do hypnosis only about 40% of the time, and the rest of the day I see clients in groups and individual and family therapy (when not providing training and supervision, or attending meetings that put me to sleep better than any induction).

HYPNOSIS AS ADJUNCT

Good therapists should have several tools in their toolbox in addition to hypnosis. When I see clients for hypnosis it is usually as part of a larger treatment program. A client I see with generalized anxiety disorder (GAD) is often concurrently treated with medication prescribed by his psychiatrist, and he may also be in individual or group therapy, including substance abuse treatment. I may be doing family therapy, and during the process I'll ask a colleague to provide some sessions of hypnosis to a family member. I may be doing conventional talk therapy with a client and at some point I will provide brief hypnosis to supplement the therapy. Clients referred by the pain clinic are always receiving *other* medical and psychological treatment,. and my provision of brief hypnotic treatment is an *adjunct.*

I work in two settings, the Department of Veterans Affairs, a health care system with munificent resources compared to much of the world, and also at a place with few resources, the refugee clinic at the University of Arizona where I do the same work (volunteer) but on a smaller scale. In both places what I do is almost always an *adjunct* to other treatment. Whether you are in private practice or work as part of an organization, I encourage you to think of hypnosis as an *adjunct* rather than as a complete treatment by itself.

WHICH CLIENTS ARE LIKELY TO BENEFIT FROM HYPNOSIS?

The bread-and-butter applications for hypnosis are anxiety disorders and chronic pain. These disorders and insomnia comprise most of my hypnosis clients. The condition that has the strongest empirical evidence for hypnotic treatment is irritable bowel syndrome (Gonsalkorale, Houghton and Whorwell, 2002; Houghton, Heyman, & Whorwell, 1996). Some dermatologic conditions, such as warts, respond very well to hypnosis (Spanos, Williams, & Glynn, 1990). There is some empirical support for the use of hypnosis in smoking cessation (Lambe, Osier, & Franks 1986) and weight loss (Barbasz & Spiegel, 1989), but only when hypnosis is an *adjunct* to other modalities. There is a vast literature on the efficacy of hypnosis in medicine, surgery, dentistry, chronic pain, and anxiety disorders, ranging from randomized clinical trials to case reports. You may read a complete discussion in *Hypnotic Techniques* (Gafner & Benson, 2003), among other sources.

Most clients who walk through the door will receive benefit. I see many chronic schizophrenics, a population you might think would be least likely to participate in hypnosis. These men and women are stable on medication and they want help in managing the secondary anxiety of the disorder (Gafner & Young, 1998). Just as with most clients with pain and anxiety, I usually see people with psychotic disorders three or four times, build in an anchor, or associational cue, such as a circle made with the thumb and index finger, to trigger relaxation when they need it; make them an audiotape containing an ego strengthening story, for example; and then they're done. It's quick and simple, the job is accomplished. A few clients, such as those with chronic depression or PTSD, I see longer for deeper work.

Like most practitioners, I don't use hypnotizability tests to measure hypnotic responsiveness—they're absolutely not necessary. If the client is interested and shows up, the rest is fairly easy.

WHICH CLIENTS SHOULD *NOT* RECEIVE HYPNOSIS?

I see some borderlines, especially if the goal is anxiety, pain management, or insomnia, as opposed to deeper work. I keep it brief, two to three sessions, and keep it concrete, here and now, with no age progression, and definitely no age regression. As with schizophrenics, borderlines seek assistance for the anxiety that can't be controlled with medication or dialectical behavior group therapy. Hypnotic ego strengthening can be very soothing and empowering, and I use it with many populations.

I never treat clients who desire exploration of "past lives." What about people who want a "magic bullet," such as, "hypnotize me so I won't be hungry"? Never. Usually these clients are not so obvious. That's why with *all* clients I have them communicate in trance right from the start; for example, "*When* you can visualize yourself in a pleasant place, any place at all, maybe walking along the beach, at home or elsewhere, let me know by nodding your head." When I've made it that easy for them and they don't respond, quite possibly they're looking for a magic bullet.

I sometimes treat clients for smoking cessation, weight management, and substance use disorders, but only if they are seriously involved in a larger program. In doing hypnosis you want to engage people in a cooperative venture, and a major way to do this is to have them communicate in trance with a head nod, finger signal, or verbal report. I also ask them to begin practicing self-hypnosis right from the start. As with conventional psychotherapy, if people "forget" to comply with a homework assignment, they may not be ready for therapy and I don't want to waste their time or mine.

UNCONSCIOUSLY DIRECTED HYPNOSIS

Hypnosis practitioners have at their disposal a panoply of techniques that go far beyond improved sleep and the management of anxiety and chronic pain. Using chronic PTSD as an example, hypnosis can assist early on with the containment of toxic stress. I often do several sessions of metaphorical ego-strengthening to help stabilize the client. Then, I usually follow with a variety of unconsciously directed techniques that can address the restructuring or reframing of traumatic experience. Again, we should think of this treatment as an *adjunct* to medication, support group, substance abuse treatment, anger management class, vocational counseling, assertiveness training, or any number of interventions.

Science has demonstrated that unconscious or automatic processes account for more of a person's mental functioning than was previously believed (Bargh & Chartrand, 1999). In other words, much of a person's everyday life is determined not by deliberate choice or conscious intention, but by features of the environment that operate outside of conscious awareness and guidance. In this book I argue for not discussing a metaphor contained in an induction, the rationale being that the metaphor may be more effective if allowed to "percolate" without conscious interference.

Work by social psychology researchers lends support to the idea of trusting one's unconscious instead of relying on conscious attention in problem solving (Dijksterhuis, Bos, Nordgren, & Van Baaren, 2006). They found that in many simple choices, such as selecting towels, conscious thought produced better results. However, for choices in more complex matters, such as deciding which house or automobile to buy, subjects who left the decision to unconscious thought made better decisions than those who relied on attentive deliberation.

Think of an archer who is aiming at that familiar target with concentric circles and a bull's eye in the middle. All of a sudden the bull's eye enlarges and now it takes up 70% of the target. In psychotherapy, how can we miss that enhanced bull's eye? A cognitive-behavioral therapist who supplements treatment with metaphor, such as anecdote or story, is taking aim at that bull's eye with several extra arrows in his quiver. So, too, the hypnosis practitioner takes aim at that bull's eye but with some vital differences: the advantage of expectancy and receptivity in trance, along with many more arrows in his quiver.

Clients in trance often readily self-reference metaphors, especially stories and anecdotes. In metaphorical ego strengthening, for example, I offer the client an example of *someone else* who has overcome a problem, or a story about a tree in the forest which has overcome adversity and gone on to survive and prevail. These are potent unconscious communications that get in "underneath the radar," interventions that empower and strengthen. In the case of PTSD, I usually build a foundation with ego strengthening before proceeding with abreactive or other techniques. People who are "stuck" may be successfully perturbed by instigative stories. For a complete discussion of these and other story techniques, such as a story within a story, alternating stories, or a story without an ending, please see *Hypnotic Techniques* (Gafner & Benson, 2003) or *Clinical Applications of Hypnosis* (Gafner, 2004).

HOW DO YOU PREPARE CLIENTS FOR HYPNOSIS?

To a large extent clients should have most of their questions answered by the time they arrive at the first session. I always elicit any negative stereotypes they may have (e.g., "Will I quack like a duck?"), answer any questions they may have, and then ask them if they are ready to begin. If I sense any reluctance, I *always* restrain them (e.g., "Perhaps you'd like to think about it before we begin, and that's okay"). Most people are ready to begin and we start right in.

GETTING STARTED WITH HYPNOSIS

It is important to offer clients a range of choices. For example, "Do you want to sit in the recliner or in a straight-back chair?" Or, "As a background sound, do you want ocean waves or rain on the sound machine, or perhaps you would like the CD of wind chimes music, or maybe nothing at all?" I remind them, "Remember, this first time we aim for a nice, comfortable experience, nothing beyond that," and invariably clients respond with a host of hypnotic phenomena, such as time distortion, dissociation, or amnesia, all of which are embedded in the inductions.

HOW DO INDUCTIONS HELP A PERSON ACHIEVE TRANCE?

For the most part, people respond because they are *ready* to respond. They want some help for their problem and they have shown up for the appointment. Aside from client readiness, or response attentiveness, four major components foster the induction of trance: (1) a comfortable, quiet setting; (2) the therapist's voice; (3) embedded suggestion; and (4) hypnotic language.

We all have a conversational voice, that is casual and relaxed. As therapists, we also have our therapeutic voice, clear and with good enunciation, perhaps employing a serious tone and lower volume to emphasize key points. Then, we have our *hypnotic voice*, clear and melodious with alternating volume, pitch, and rate. I employ a near whisper to emphasize key suggestions, keeping in mind that a subtle vocal shift is thought to be an unconscious communication. The late Bob Hall was fond of saying, "Massage 'em with your voice." Through practice, you find your *hypnotic voice.* When you hear the term *embedded suggestion,* you may be asking, "Embed? Is this like a reporter in a war zone *embedded* with an Army unit?" Well, kind of: Embedded suggestion, a major technique in hypnosis, may be delivered several ways. For example, words containing *in*, such as *in*ward and ima*gin*ation, convey internal search or process, as does the pun, "an entrance into another state." I might also tell a story about someone else who "embarked on a journey of discovery where *intuition* turned out to be a most remarkable resource. . . . " In these examples, listeners in trance have heightened receptivity to suggestion and metaphor, and are likely to incorporate them in their own unique way. Each induction in this book draws heavily on embedded suggestion, especially suggestions of hypnotic phenomena, such as dissociation, time distortion, and amnesia. These phenomena are what we want people to experience in trance. It is the *experiencing* that convinces clients that they have achieved trance, so in the debriefing portion of the procedure we ratify these phenomena; for example, in reinforcing time distortion, we ask, "Looking at the clock on the wall, do you think that *more* time has passed or *less* since you came in here?" Or, with dissociation, we ask, "How do you feel in your hands and your feet?" If they answer with, "My hands feel kind of numb," we know that they have experienced anesthesia. If they say that their hands—or their feet—feel disconnected from their body, they have experienced dissociation. If they can't remember all or part of an induction, or a story, that's amnesia.

Hypnotic language is a potent ally of the therapist and drives the induction. Here are some examples:

"*Those* hands of yours, hands *up*   *dissociative language*
there, or feet *down* below, I can   *apposition of opposites*
imagine, or other *wonder when*   *power words: implication*
you will begin to experience a *tin-*
gling or *numbness, heaviness* or   *apposition of opposites*
lightness, coolness or *warmth,* or   *suggestion covering all*
maybe *some other* curious sensa-   *possibilities*
tion somewhere . . . , *and* then that   *linking word*
feeling can spread out, really
slowing down your mind and
body both. . . . "

COMPONENTS OF A SESSION

I divide a hypnosis session into five components: *Pretrance work discussion*, where clients "check in" and report on their practice to date of the technique; the *induction* phase, where the therapist helps them achieve trance; *deepening*, where their experience is deepened, for example, with counting down from 10 to 1; the *therapy component*, which could be an ego strengthening story, age regression to discover past mastery, or any other number of techniques; *realerting*, commonly, "I'm going to count now from one up to five and when I reach three or four you may realert yourself as if waking up from a nice, refreshing nap"; and finally *debriefing*, where the therapist inquires about hypnotic phenomena achieved, thus ratifying the experience, and asks what was useful and what was not.

In debriefing you may learn that clients could not hear you, that they were distracted by the mention of their name, or anything else that was helpful or not.

It is important to remain flexible and attend to the person's needs. As such, the procedure is individualized to each client. If, for example, there is a crisis or something pressing, it may be best to forego hypnosis that day and "just talk." In terms of the induction, deepening, and therapy phases, we should remember that these are but artificial divisions. I have found that therapists new to hypnosis learn best by dividing the session into clearly definable units. However, many practitioners make no such distinctions, and instead blend all phases together. I encourage you to experiment and find what works best for you and your clients.

At the beginning of each session you should tell the client what you have planned that day. If you say, "Today, I plan on leading you through an age regression exercise in order to learn when you last felt good about yourself," and if, nonverbally (or verbally) the client shows reluctance, then maybe you need to reach for plan B. Also, whenever I plan to employ a confusional technique, I tell them ahead of time, "Some things you hear today may not make conscious sense. I'm doing this to get in underneath your radar, to help you." A good doctor does not prescribe bad medicine (Papp, 1983), and you can't go wrong by framing something as helpful.

SEEDING

Seeding is a technique that I often employ as part of the hypnosis. Think of foreshadowing in a book or movie: If the writer has inserted dark storm clouds or you hear a clap of thunder, very often this portends something sinister. In therapy, if I intend to tell a client a story about *slowing down,* I may seed the idea ahead of time by casually mentioning the *slow* traffic driving to work. Or, I may nonverbally seed the idea by *slowly* getting up to get my notebook. It is believed that by seeding a concept ahead of time you prepare the client to receive the idea when the seed is activated. This is similar to priming in social psychology. In experiments to influence choice of laundry detergent, subjects who were primed with ocean and moon were more likely to select Tide (Geary, 1994).

HOW TO USE THIS BOOK

This book has five chapters, each covering a different type of induction: "Story Inductions," "Inductions for Sleep," "Inductions for Children," "Directive Inductions," and "Confusional Inductions." For the majority of adults, story inductions will be sufficient to induce trance. Some of these inductions, such as the sleep induction, were designed to address insomnia; however, they can be used for problems other than insomnia. All of the story inductions include the liberal use of hypnotic phenomena (Edgette & Edgette, 1995). The aim, of course, is for clients to experience these phenomena, because that's what trance is all about.

The legacy of hypnosis is directive or authoritarian inductions, and as many people still practice in this fashion, you may feel more comfortable with this approach. If the client achieves trance with a story or directive induction, good, your job is done. However, some clients, mainly because of unconscious resistance, are unable to achieve trance with story inductions or directive inductions. They want to go into trance, but just can't do it. That's when you reach for a confusional induction, which works most of the time. It is estimated that 10% of the U.S. population is nonhypnotizable. In my experience this percentage can be halved through the use of confusional inductions.

Hypnosis with children in many ways is much more interesting than hypnosis with adults. Children are usually more unburdened and spontaneous, so practitioners have available to them multitudinous routes to trance. In the chapter on children you are offered some examples of these routes.

I encourage you to mix and match the various inductions and deepenings in this book. As you try out different approaches you will discover which best suits you and your clients.

2

Story Inductions

Inductions similar to the ones in this chapter have previously been referred to as conversational or embedded meaning inductions. Each one employs a story, or a story within a story, so I am calling them story inductions. They rely heavily on suggestions for hypnotic phenomena, which are embedded in the induction.

DISSOCIATION

Yapko noted, "Clinically the induction serves as a vehicle for facilitating the dissociation that defines hypnotic experience, as well as building responsiveness to the suggestions yet to come" (2005, p. 108). Dissociation occurs naturally with or without trance, and may refer to a person's mental or physical experience functioning distinctly and independently from another part. This experience may entail the person's mentally dividing visual images from emotions; separating one part of the body from another part; feeling an overall detachment from the immediate physical environment; or, at its extreme, perceiving two or more separate personalities sharing one mind (Edgette & Edgette, 1995).

Dissociation Induction

You may sit back and close your eyes, if you wish, as I read you the following story. We had a client one time who had a degree of difficulty distancing herself from past events. "Have you ever experienced dissociation?" I asked her. "Dissociation?" she answered. "Yes," I said, "you know, that rather puzzling phenomenon whereby part of a person, or all of the person, experiences an amused detachment. Detachment is the key." "Well, I don't know if I can do that," she answered. However, after a session or two, that *woman* surprised herself with her response.

metaphor

One time there was a man named Will Trilling, and I said to him, "Will, won't you sit back, and listen to the following words that have been carefully pieced together to help you achieve a degree of *detachment?*" He nodded his head and I proceeded. "Now, Will, you need to know beforehand that *some*, or *part*, of the following may not make perfect sense, but let me assure you that the *purpose* of this story is to help you relax, fully and completely, and to *let go*, so that you can *dissociate* in your own unique way."

dissociation

rationale

suggestion

I continued talking to Will. He had taken one nice, deep refreshing breath, and no doubt he surprised himself at how quickly he could settle into that chair, *effortlessly, without even trying, involuntarily . . . unconsciously.* Just observing him I could see that he was beginning to lose himself in some private reverie, drifting off in his own special way, and I hoped that part of him was still paying attention to the vital task at hand. I could see that his conscious mind was aroused as my words continued. "Will, way up high in a space station with no gravity, a dinner plate will float, and beneath the ocean we have tectonic plates, whose shifting may be of gravity. There's the North Pole, the South Pole, this hemisphere and that, land and sea, great *distances* some places, short *spans* in other places. I'd like you to *imagine* now, Will, just *imagine* a map, or a globe, and there you see the roads, rivers, borders, mountains, one thing *extending* to another, another *reaching* to here, there *stretching* to that; for example, a bridge *spreads* from bank to bank, or spans from shore to shore.

"The causeway from New Orleans to Mandeville *must have a reason*, even though the other side is far-off, remote. One traveler said, 'It's *outlying, far away,* or *ulterior,*' and her traveling companion, already several steps ahead of her, in her mind, responded, 'No, it's clear off *over there*, nearly abroad, *farther* more than further,' and the discussion was only *truncated* by the first traveler who

suggestion covering all possibilities

dissociation

power word

dissociation

fluff

dissociation

dissociation

remarked, '*Irregardless* may be a double nega- *fluff*
tive, and we can hear well with both ears, even
though anyone's hearing with their *third ear* is *suggestion*
far superior.'"

By now Will was probably *tuning out* the
words, and I could only imagine the extent to
which one hand, or the other, had begun to
experience some curious sensation. Looking *negative hallucination*
at Will just then I could guess that sensations
in his extremities were highly *quizzical/physi-* *misspeak*
cal indeed. Perhaps his legs already felt
detached from the rest of him, I did not know, *dissociation*
and it really didn't matter, as I told him, "Will,
did you ever have a leg, or a foot, *fall asleep,* *analgesia*
during a long, boring drive?" He nodded
imperceptibly and I added, "A person can
relax, really slow down, and you don't need
those hands or *those* feet, and you can always *dissociative language*
be in the *driver's seat.*" Will's breathing was *metaphor*
now even and regular, and he may have even
fallen asleep.

I continued addressing my words to Will
though from my vantage point I could have
been a very distant voice. "Will, isn't it nice to *suggestion*
really *slow down*? There is fast and slow, *slow* *apposition of opposites*
and *fast*, with various velocities in between,
and we had this person one time, his name
was Ben, Ben from Israel, and he liked to drive
fast. He said, 'I really feel like I'm *somewhere*
else when I'm cruising down the road.' A few
months back he got stopped for speeding, and
the cop said to him, 'Beginning now you can
just imagine, Ben, how your checking account
will feel lighter after you're *separated* from that
one hundred and fifteen dollars.' And ever

after, Ben slowed down, but just to seven miles over the speed limit, and his whole body experienced a most enjoyable *disconnectedness.*"

dissociation

I asked Will to nod his head one more time if he was still *immersed in an image*, driving down the road, or any image at all, and his right index finger twitched ever so slightly, which, of course, I took as a yes. "Will, when you're watching a movie you unwittingly *tune out* a distraction, like some inconsiderate whispering behind you. Not hearing the whispering may be called a negative hallucination, a highly positive thing, but it can also be termed as *dissociating* the distraction. Come to think of it, daily life requires such dissociation because if a person *associated* to everything you would have to tell yourself, when walking, for example, 'pick up the right foot, now the left foot' and so on. When Will was realerted later, one foot, I forget which, felt *quite apart* from his leg. 'It's *parceled out* over there' were his words. He then added, 'Myself, or maybe just my leg, is *optimistic/up to mischief.*'" But that was at the end of the story and we're not quite there yet.

suggestion

negative hallucination

dissociation

misspeak

In the 1800s Pierre Janet discussed amnesia in trance, and thought of it not as a matter of *just forgetting*, but rather like information *kept apart* in another part of the mind. When reading a story to Will, his focused concentration on the words . . . and the voice . . . reflected his dissociation from all else in the immediate environment. In that story to Will, one time, the person in the story had a special talent for *spacing out* during the day, something Will did

amnesia
dissociation

dissociation

not remember once he was awakened from   *amnesia*
trance.

"I told Will about someone I saw once who
associated too much, that is, she worried
excessively, and it kept her awake at night.
This ruminator successfully imagined her
thoughts *sectioned off* in an adjacent room,   *dissociation*
but only during the night when she didn't need
them. 'Play *gin rummy* with each other in the
next room,' she told them. Another person   *dissociation*
with disapproving thoughts learned to keep
them *at mental bay*, probably because she
grew up on a farm where baying and lowing
were part of everyday life.

I was certain that Will had definitely *drifted*   *suggestion*
off to sleep, and when I touched his shoe to
awaken him, he opened his eyes with a start
and said, "Can metaphor be a *bridge to experi-*   *suggestion*
ence?" which really distracted me at the time,
but now when I drive on expansion bridges I'd
rather be in a tunnel.   *lead away*

10–1 Deepening

Beginning now, (client's name), I'd like you to let your experience develop
and further deepen as I count backward from ten down to one, 10 . . . 9 . . .

Clinical Comments

Three potent, unconscious communication techniques are subtle vocal
shift, lead away, and misspeak. In a story, I will alter my voice slightly for
key suggestions; for example, " . . . and all those balloons, she *just let them
go.*" With lead away, a suggestion is offered, and it is followed by a non
sequitur or distracting statement. I often employ lead away with clients
who tend to analyze content. With misspeak, I offer a suggestion, which is

quickly followed by the supposedly intended word. For example, "Darlene dearly loved animals, cats, dogs, gerbils, guinea pigs and other animals, but she came to realize that a person doesn't need to hang onto any bad *habits/rabbits*." With misspeak and lead away, I don't want to overdo it. Two or three times is usually enough.

Dissociation is perhaps the most versatile hypnotic phenomenon. Suggestions that employ dissociation may include such things as, for example, while undergoing an MRI procedure, "Your mind can be in the parking lot while your body is in the machine." Or, during surgery, "Your right hand can experience a dull sensation during surgery while any discomfort can take place in your left big toe." With social phobia, "When around others any fear that may arise can conveniently play itself out around the corner." To foster a conscious/unconscious split, say in unconscious problem solving, you may suggest, "Your conscious mind can pay attention to the words while your unconscious mind seeks new ways to solve the problem." The conscious/unconscious split can be seeded early on with something like, "The famous doctor in Phoenix years ago, Milton Erickson, said, 'A person's conscious mind is smart, but her unconscious mind is much wiser.'" Cade and O'Hanlon (1993) offer a thorough discussion of such pattern interruption, something we refer to as O'Hanlon's List (Gafner & Benson, 2003). This approach posits that the therapist is usually more successful in *transforming* the symptom rather than trying to eliminate it.

A facility for dissociation is inherent in certain disorders, such as PTSD. I frame this to the client as a hypnotic talent; for example, "We can build on your natural ability to detach and space out." Accordingly, the above induction may be apt, but not always. Some people with a fragile sense of control may feel distressed at experiencing dissociation so strongly. If I sense a control issue, I may use only a portion of the Dissociation induction, perhaps combining it with another induction. If the person responds positively, I may use this induction on subsequent occasions. Remember: with any induction you are testing the client's response. The induction *sets up* the deepening and therapy components. Remember, when you take a boat to an island for a vacation, the island is your destination, not the boat.

TIME DISTORTION

Time distortion may involve time expansion or time contraction, and a client may be told, "For a person in trance, time may seem to slow down or speed up. . . ." In any induction we want to liberally employ hypnotic phenomena,and then ratify it later during debriefing; for example, "Oh, so it seems like *more* time has passed rather than less. Very good." The more people realize that they have experienced hypnotic phenomena, the more they become invested in the process. These convincers of trance reinforce the idea that the procedure will help them with their problem.

Clocks Induction

Beginning now, I'd like you to settle into that chair, and you may close your eyes if you wish, as I tell you a story having to do with time, yes, time.

She had the curious name of Secondhand and in her youth she endured jokes about her name, and was called things like Hand-Me-Down, Hour Hand, and who knows what else? Secondhand was her name and I never knew if it was her first name, middle, last, or just a nickname, and it really doesn't matter, as this story is about her lecture one day at the historical society, a lecture on her favorite topic, the history of clocks, which she often referred to as timekeepers.

Secondhand arrived late and she began her talk by announcing, "Whenever I give this lecture after lunch like this some people *doze off, dream and drift in their own way*, or actually *fall asleep*, and I won't take it personally if you do any of those things.

suggestion covering all possibilities

"Timekeepers can be designed to show absolute time, as in the 'the talk began at 17 minutes past 3:00, or at 15:17, if that's your preference.' Or, a timekeeper can show elapsed time, as in 'the speaker went on for two hours and 45 minutes.' Those of you here today may have a watch, a phone, or some other modern device that provides the time, but I prefer to listen to the bell towers chime on the hour, but when I'm home I listen to one of my grandfather clocks announce various intervals of time. Some chime every half hour, some every quarter hour, but only one chimes on the hour."

I looked at my watch as Secondhand continued. We settled into our chairs now, each of us beginning to *become absorbed* in some aspect of time past or time present, with little regard for future time. Suddenly Secondhand whispered, "I'm going to divulge the most curious aspect of clocks, but not just yet."

suggestion

Slides on the screen showed sundials, candle clocks, hourglasses, and lamp clocks. She passed around a square object, its case of lacquered brass and glass. "This rare item is an eight-day carriage clock made in France in 1803," she said. My mind, now a misty sea of memory, drifted to Napolean and Hornblower, and her words were but *distant utterances* absorbed by the room.

dissociation

"What about atomic clocks and crystal-oscillator clocks?" asked a woman from somewhere behind me. "Madam, you may *contemplate, imagine,* or even *wonder* about and even become immersed in, sophisticated timekeepers, but they are beyond the scope of this talk," answered Secondhand. "What is this most 'curious aspect' you alluded to?" asked a man in front. "Ah, you must listen very closely to glean the most curious, but now is not the time," she responded.

power words

The lecture continued. I closed my eyes as the words *danced* overhead and *floated* off to

dissociation

one side of the room: "Evidence suggests that mechanical clocks first appeared shortly before, or after, 1297 A.D., and continued until 1650, give or take mere months or years, and they were erratic and imprecise, which explains why precision in terms of time in those days was of little import."

A person behind me whispered, "Time, time as we perceive it, time in our minds, time on any clock, is an *elusive phenomenon*." I don't   *time distortion* know how the lecturer heard him, but in mid-sentence she paused, stared in our direction, and declared, "Elusive or an illusion, I have pondered both from time to time."

Even though I was striving to pay close attention, my *dreamlike state* had now deep-   *suggestion* ened, and my mind enjoyed a particular levity, journeying from *here* to *there* and back again,   *apposition of opposites* while my body, operating quite *independently*,   *dissociation* was overtaken by a most enjoyable heaviness. If my legs had not quite *fallen asleep*, why was   *analgesia* it so difficult to move them?   *direct question*

I remember consciously deciding at the time that feelings in my body, or the dreaming of my mind, or anything else occurring in those seconds and minutes, did not matter at all, as I breathed deeply and let my overall experience develop. Thinking about it *later*, and especially *now*, that was certainly a most   *apposition of opposites* satisfying interval of time. The woman to my right was typing steadily on her laptop. Whether my body was listing her way, or if I leaned in her direction to look, I *cannot recall*,   *amnesia* but I do remember the words on her screen: "*Nothing to know*, nothing to do, nowhere to   *not knowing/not doing* be, no one to please, *no expectations to meet,* and you don't even have to pay conscious attention to anything at all."

Those words brought a smile to my lips, and just then Secondhand's words resounded in the room: "Mechanical clocks require a source of energy, as all timekeepers mark the passage of time by allowing energy to dissipate at a controlled rate, and the device that permits this action is called an *escapement.*" *suggestion* Soon the man's whisper appeared again: 'You look like you've *escaped* on a journey already." Someone near the back crept out of the room.

I glanced again at the laptop screen and read, "nothing to know, nothing to do . . . ," and then the words disappeared from the screen. I heard the man whisper again, "*Escape* is very *suggestion* pleasant. . . . " As I tried to make sense of it all the lecturer's words appeared again: "Up until the first decade of the 19th century all clocks in America and Europe were produced by *individual* craftsmen. Each clock was an *inde-* *pendent* project, and quite *separately* joiners, *dissociation* turners, metalworkers, and others contributed their *parts* to produce a complete clock. The industry, on the other hand . . . ," and Second-hand's words trailed off.

The room was silent now. The laptop was closed and sat on the chair once occupied by the woman. Others in the room were *immo-* *catalepsy* *bile,* eyes closed, chins on their chests. I noticed a Latino man in the chair to my left. He smiled, looked down at my right hand, and uttered, "I have my hand, and you have that left hand, *que no?*" *direct question*

In front, the lecturer intoned, "By looking at you, half asleep, or completely *asleep*, I must reveal that it has taken me many years of practice to become this boring. And now might be a good time to talk about pendulum clocks." With that, she took out a large pendulum. She set it on the table and it rhythmically moved back and forth, back and forth, and once again I closed my eyes. This time I went even deeper, drifting and dreaming into a most pleasant state. (Shaffer, 1980)

suggestion

Silent Deepening

I'm going to be quiet for a few minutes. You can let your experience develop and deepen, and I'll resume speaking again in a while.

Clinical comments

Clients usually experience time distortion, but not always. It is uncanny how we can emphasize one hypnotic phenomenon and people experience *another* phenomenon, such as amnesia that may have been mentioned only briefly.

I knew a therapist who went to great lengths to foster time distortion. He usually seeded it at the start of the session by mentioning how, for example, "I lost track of time this morning and got here late," or "My watch stopped and then started again." He even had three clocks hanging on the walls of his office, all with different times. "Yes, I'll get to it some time," he answered when people commented on the variance.

AMNESIA

In hypnosis, it is normal for clients to forget at least a portion of what they hear, or experience, during the session. Why would a therapist want to *foster* amnesia? First, it is very gratifying for a client to experience amnesia, as the experience is a strong convincer of trance. Second, for therapists whose primary thrust is unconscious, we *want* people to *not* consciously remember key suggestions, as some of us believe that hypnosis is more effective if unconscious processing proceeds without conscious interference. Certainly discussing the procedure following realerting may serve to undermine this effect.

However, others argue for discussion of key suggestions or metaphors, trusting less in the benevolent wisdom of the unconscious. To be sure, if I'm working with a sociopath, or a very concrete person, I may opt for discussion.

Amnesia Induction

As you sit back and listen to the following story, you *may experience* trance in a way that recalls   *implication* something from the past, a pleasant and memorable occasion when you felt a particular freedom or *letting go*, perhaps more in your mind   *suggestion* than your body, or vice versa. If you're like most people, many things from the past have *escaped memory*, and by the time I'm done reading this story you may quite possibly have *no conscious*   *amnesia* *recollection* of some details that you intended to remember, which is just fine, because the main thing is to just sit back, close those eyes if you wish, and listen to a story about *Wendel*, who   *metaphor* went to work every day at the library.

Wendel didn't work on any of the main floors of the library. He didn't work where hundreds of people bustled about quietly amidst the shelves of books and the computer terminals. He worked in the basement, down there in the Erickson Archives, where they kept books like O'Hanlon's 1901 *For Want of a Perturbable Condition*, Edgette's *Mutative Intervention Chronicles* from

1791, and Yapko's *Autonomous Amnesia Review*, complete volumes from 1813 to 1821, or an 1830 copy of *Haley's Regrets*, one of his favorite books, though each time he read it he discovered something peculiar that he would later *forget*. Down there, Wendel would experience a *reverie* and delightful *detachment* from the everyday world. Five o'clock would come and his boss would gently touch his shoulder and say, "Wake up, Wendel, time to go home," and invariably Wendel would look up to see his hand holding a pencil, *suspended* in the air, or he would discover his legs had fallen *asleep*. "What the deuce?!" he would answer, as he had completely *lost track of time*. In time, his boss, or those who followed through the years, came to say simply, "Wake up, Deuce."

amnesia
suggestion
dissociation

catalepsy
analgesia

time distortion

But Wendel wasn't simply a dreamer. He worked diligently all day long among the Archives, but at the same time his mind *drifted and dreamed*, and often he pondered his English class *back in high school*, and his teacher, Miss Bernadette Givings. He vividly recalled *Miss Givings's* class, the first period after lunch, when all the students were *drowsy* and inattentive.

suggestion

age regression
pun

suggestion

"Who left this apple on my desk?" Miss Givings would ask. "I don't know" answered Enrique. "I *forgot*," responded Wendel. "Sure you did," smiled Miss Givings. One time Miss Givings set up a video camera in her classroom, and after finding two apples on her desk and hearing Wendel say he *forgot*, she played the tape for the class, and sure enough, there was Wendel, stealing in, setting down the apples. "What have you to say now?" she asked. "The proof is on the tape, but

amnesia

amnesia

frankly I *don't remember* any of it," responded Wendel. Other times, after finding an apple or two and playing the tape, she would simply say, "Wendel, you can *remember to forget or forget to remember*, the choice is yours," words that were now *unforgetably memorable* in Wendel's imagination. Sometimes she would say, "Wendel, you're a very *good forgetter*," and the other students frequently told him, "*You sure have Miss Givings*." "I don't have Miss Givings, not by a long shot," he answered.

amnesia

pun/fluff

    In deep contemplation now in the Archives he was especially absorbed in the brittle pages of some antiquated tome. He eyes settled on the word *immersion* and his dreamlike state deepened. His body was made of *lead*, or so it seemed, heavy and *unable to move*, while his mind was *unyielding*, as any world beyond the word *immersion* ceased to exist.

suggestion
catalepsy

suggestion

    Miss Givings eventually stopped videotaping because everyone knew who the culprit was; however, the ritual continued: finding apples on the desk, asking who put them there, and the inevitable *forgetting*. One time Miss Givings began to speak to Wendel, and after stopping abruptly, she held out her hand as if to shake Wendel's. Wendel's hand went out to meet hers, but Miss Givings pulled her hand back, leaving Wendel's *suspended in the air*. "You may *not remember* this experience," she whispered. However, years later, he remembered it well.

catalepsy
amnesia

    "*You sure have Miss Givings*," he was constantly reminded by the others, and he always retorted, "*I don't have Miss Givings* at all." However, you know how it is when people tell you

fluff

something so many times, that eventually you begin to wonder.

At times, after finding an apple or two on her desk, she would ask Wendel to approach the front of the class. "Sit here in this chair, young man," she commanded. She continued, "Wendel, close those eyes and let your mind become occupied by an apple, red or green, large or small, any apple will do; and your conscious mind may lose sight of your body, and you can *put out of mind*   *negative hallucination* the sound of my voice, the chair supporting your body, as well as everyone in this room, and beginning now, Wendel, *sleep*, yes, sleep, very deeply."   *suggestion*

The rest of the class also fell asleep that day, and when the bell rang they awakened to find their teacher calmly biting into an apple. "Don't tell me about Miss Givings," Wendel announced to his classmates. Ruth, the smartest girl in the class, took him aside out in the hall and said, "It's okay to *forget* Miss Givings or anything else, Wendel."   *amnesia*

Mr. Holt's Horse: Deepening

You may allow your experience to deepen while I recount a most memorable event that occurred in the Canadian Rockies in 1883. C. S. Holt was riding his horse on a narrow mountain trail when the horse slipped, and both horse and rider fell 75 feet to a ledge above the raging river below. Holt was pulled to safety, but the horse, after struggling to its feet, tumbled down to the river and disappeared downstream.

A few days later the horse was found, with only one eye, broken legs and other serious injuries. Holt insisted on sparing its life, and over several weeks it was nursed back to health. A year later a soldier was seen riding a one-eyed horse, and observers confirmed that it was indeed Mr. Holt's horse (Steele, 1883).

Clinical Comments

After offering an induction laden with embedded suggestions, a deepening in the form of a straightforward story may seem like a welcome respite to clients. As they listen to the story, clients often *consciously* search for meaning, which allows deepening to occur on an unconscious level. As such, an overall deeper experience can result compared to a conventional deepening, such as counting from 10 to one.

A few years back I saw a man named Humberto. He had been arrested for a crime, which turned out to be a case of mistaken identity. Nevertheless, the damage had been done: His name had appeared in the local newspaper, and "Now," he said, "Everybody stares at me and I can't get it out of my mind."

Many things were tried to stem his incessant ruminations: medication and conventional talk therapy; a paradoxical directive, where he was instructed to schedule his worrying; and then hypnosis, with indirect techniques and suggestions for letting go. None of these interventions helped. However, during hypnosis I noted that Humberto experienced a marked amnesia for all content. Now, in talking to the client I gathered some very useful information about his daily activity. During the next hypnosis session, I told him: "On your daily drive, when you cross Mormon Road by the railroad tracks, *something will come to you* that will help you with this problem. However, you will forget that I even mentioned this to you."

When he returned two weeks later, he was calm and happy. "I no longer have those thoughts in my mind," he reported. "Are you doing anything different?" I asked. "Yes," he answered, "I'm using that anchor and practicing my deep breathing."

He had not seen fit to employ the anchor and deep breathing before, but now he was doing so. Unconscious problem solving had occurred and he had no conscious awareness of the process. That was the last time I saw him. He has not returned to the clinic and 15 years have now passed.

There are a host of ways to foster amnesia, ranging from the direct (e.g., "Beginning now you may conveniently forget anything you may have intended to remember"), to the metaphorical (e.g., "I slept last night and dreamed, and when I awoke I could remember only a small portion of my dream"), to the sublime, "You can't possibly remember everything in your conscious mind" (Zeig, 1985b, p. 329).

A distraction is one of the best ways to foster amnesia. I will realert the client and immediately begin talking about the weather, or something else irrelevant. For a thorough discussion of amnesia see *Hypnotic Techniques* (Gafner & Benson, 2000).

Let's not forget that amnesia is not a magic bullet. In Humberto's case, *change* occurred because it was contingent on tagging it to naturally occurring behavior, and his unconscious had been provided with some concrete resources, mainly the anchor and deep breathing. Humberto did not require further talk therapy for purposes of conscious integration, but many clients might require precisely that.

CATALEPSY

When trance subjects experience catalepsy they feel immobile in one or more parts of the body (Edgette & Edgette, 1995). Kroger (1963) defined the phenomenon as involuntary tonicity of the muscles and Erickson and Rossi (1981) defined the phenomenon as a suspension of voluntary movement and a condition of well-balanced tonicity. With children as an exception, clients in trance usually evince very little movement, if at all, along with a "facial mask," and little swallowing. When we ask them to rehearse their anchor (e.g., "Right now I want you to touch together that thumb and first finger on your right hand, forming a little circle"), the hand is often very heavy and movement requires considerable effort.

Catalepsy has value as an important phenomenon to be ratified, but it also has indications in therapy. Body stillness during medical and surgical procedures may be a goal, just as "stillness and calmness of both your mind and body" may be a target in anxiety disorders of both children and adults. Edgette and Edgette (1995) have employed catalepsy for restlessness and pain control of women awaiting delivery in childbirth. I have found the phenomenon to be of considerable utility for people undergoing opthalmologic and dental procedures, as well as for chronic pain and insomnia.

Edgette and Edgette use unconscious/conscious dissociative suggestions; for example, "Your conscious mind can be quite active in thinking while your unconscious mind promotes physical stillness" (p. 179, 1995). Employing metaphor, the Edgettes (1995) draw on examples like Tchaikovsky's *Nutcracker Suite*. In this ballet, toys are unmoving and suddenly come to life on cue. When I work with children I draw attention to the flexible but immobile qualities of the green figurine, Gumby, or use similar characteristics of animals made of modeling clay and dolls. However, such use is not limited to children. When you use them in therapy with adults you evoke an "early learning set" that may tap into long forgotten talents and abilities.

I sometimes seed a "slowing down" target by handing the client one of these toys shortly after the session has begun. "Notice the qualities of this little Gumby," I say, and then add, "I wonder what you can learn from him." At this point, if the client wishes to discuss the metaphor, I usually offer a restraining statement, such as, "Oh, don't read too much into this. Time is moving on and we need to get started with hypnosis. Last time, did we have on ocean waves or wind chimes music?"

Catalepsy Induction

You may settle into that chair and close your eyes if you wish, as I tell you about a symposium on hypnotic phenomena that occurred some years back. Two professors up on stage were enjoying a heated debate about catalepsy, that *feeling of immobility* a person may experience in trance as well as in everyday life.   *catalepsy*

A professor from the Analgesia Department remarked, "Whenever I think about the catabolic winds on a glacier I feel *numb* all over." The professor from the Anesthesia Department retorted, "Your reexperiencing numbness may be called catalepsy only if your *body stillness* is accompanied by an active and expectant mind whose *suspended awareness* leads to new perspectives."   *analgesia*

catalepsy

Analgesia took this as an insult, unclipped his microphone, and marched off the stage. His fellow debater stared after him, *mouth agape, body locked in unmovingness* for 20 seconds, 30 seconds, one minute. . . . He *didn't hear* the murmurs in the audience, and some people rose to exit. Just then an old man in a wheel chair appeared, clipped on the microphone, and asked in a gravelly voice, "Professor, I am Doctor Dissociativo. May I have your hand?" He took the professor's hand and said, "and we'll just let that hand float out there, as if it has a *mind of its own*, while we demonstrate some hypnotic phenomena, will that be okay?" Anesthesia's eyes were now closed, he nodded, and the audience became very still as they observed this sudden turn of events.

catalepsy

negative hallucination

dissociation

The doctor continued: "Professor, if you are *not* a good hypnotic subject, that arm now extended can drop down to your side." Anesthesia just stood there, *arm extended*, and while the doctor waited for a response, he addressed the audience. "Beginning now, ladies and gentlemen, I would like to enlist your participation in a little experiment, and if you would be so kind as to let your eyes close . . . that's the way . . . and you can sit back and begin to experience your very own *entrance into another state*. You can listen to my words or not, as you drift off into a most peaceful, satisfying state of relaxation, *wondering just how deeply relaxed* a person can become."

suggestion

implication

Dissociativo waved to someone offstage, and soon the lights were dimmed and soothing wind chimes music filled the auditorium.

The doctor appeared to be asleep there in his wheelchair, but after a few moments he opened his eyes and addressed Anesthesia once again: "Professor, looking at you it's hard for me to believe you're *not* a good hyp-notic subject, but I'll take you at your *arm/*word and proceed with a little script I prepared just the other day for a person in our trance labora-tory. That individual, too, "professed" to have few hypnotic talents.

misspeak

"No doubt you're familiar with the term *glad hander*, a person whose insincere hand-shakes and effusiveness might cause us to hold back *our* own hand, and any hand, *my* hand or *your* hand, may be divisible by sensa-tion parts, various feelings *here*, *there*, *this* fin-ger or *that*, *top* of hand or *bottom*, and then we have time. *Then-now-before*, presently *right* hand willing *left* hand reluctant previously unknowing tingling feeling forgotten left hand, or was it the right? *Numb* or *tingling*, *warm* or *cold*, *heavy* or *light*, then feeling before, won-der what sensation now where? A left hand immersed in frigid water forgotten in the depths of now *not feeling* anything there. Just what is it?

apposition of opposites

confusion

analgesia

"'Won't you, Will,' I said to Will, Will Knottsberry was his name, I said, 'Will, left hand can rise, *would it not?*' They called him Naturally Knott, or Natural for short. In school Natural always sat cross-legged in his chair and he was the first to have his hand in the air to answer the teacher's question, and *that* hand *stayed up there* for the longest time, as if a balloon held it up with a string, and

confusion

dissociative language
catalepsy

while waiting, waiting, Natural gazed out the window and imagined hot air balloons in the distance. He just kept that hand up there all the time, even before the next question was asked, and when it came, it was a most curious question.

"'Class,' the teacher asked, 'If you blow up a balloon and gently poke your finger into its side, *is your finger* then inside the balloon or outside the balloon?' Natural waved his hand, eager to answer, and the teacher asked, 'Will Knottsberry, have your legs fallen asleep yet?'

fluff

direct question

"That concludes my story. Kind audience and professor, in a moment I'm going to ask you to let your experience to deepen, but not just yet. Take one or two nice, comfortable breaths, and I'll resume speaking again shortly."

1–30/40–1 Deepening

(Client's name), let's have your experience deepen as we do some counting together. I'll count out loud, from one to 30, like this, 1 . . . , 2 . . . , and as I count up, I'd like you to count at the same pace, but from 40 down to 1, like this, 40 . . . , 39 . . . , but not just yet. I count up, you count down, slowly from 40, and I'll start my counting now, 1 . . . , 2 . . . .

Clinical Comments

With catalepsy, as with other phenomena, we sometimes aim for *complete* immobility, which may be unrealistic. Instead, let's allow for clients to experience *some* movement, which they will probably do anyway. If they adjust themselves in the chair, or reach up to scratch their head, I *pace* the behavior (e.g., "Even though your body is heavy you can still do anything you need to do to feel comfortable"), and then *lead*, or add on, in the desired direction (e.g., "One person one time felt like a sturdy oak tree whose flexible woodenness allowed it to bend in the wind"). So, too, with suggestions for negative hallucination. It is more realistic to suggest, "Your mind can tune out a *good portion* of your husband's criticism," rather than suggesting that her mind totally obliterate the criticism. With amnesia, we can suggest, "I wonder if you can just forget *one important aspect* of the emotional impact," thus effecting a pattern interruption.

We think of catalepsy to counter anxiety; however, it is also useful in *mirroring* the immobility of depression, lack of movement in therapy, or constipation-predominant irritable bowel syndrome. Mirroring communicates understanding, but understanding is not enough. We want to *add on* in the desired direction; for example, "This heaviness in your mind . . . and in your body . . . is one thing, and the deepest part of you knows that *movement* can now begin, perhaps slowly and almost imperceptibly at first, and then, who knows how much more *meaningful activity* will follow?"

A direct question is a simple but elegant technique that rivets attention and can be quite instigative, because it tends to stimulate associations and facilitate responsiveness. As with other techniques such as misspeak, you don't want to overdo it, and using it once or twice in an induction is usually enough.

HIDDEN OBSERVER

I use this induction for people who have control issues. In other words, they *want* to go into trance, but they have difficulty trusting and letting go. Such a difficulty may also be viewed as unconscious resistance. If they don't respond to this, I usually reach for a confusional induction.

Hidden Observer Induction

You can just sit back and close your eyes, if you wish, as I tell you a little story about someone who had a very active hidden observer, you know, that part of your mind which is neither fully conscious nor unconscious, but which observes what is going on during trance. This *person*—we'll call her Hidden—her naturally occurring observer phenomenon was very *robust and ever present* in her, and showed itself in various ways. For example, after she closed her eyes she would ask herself, "Am I doing this right?" I would answer, "That's the way, just notice your breathing and I'll be quiet for a few moments as you begin to notice your body, and what sensations or feelings develop on the inside. Those things happening on the inside are often the first indicator of trance, didn't you know?"

At the end, after she had opened her eyes, she would ask, "Was I supposed to remember everything?" "There's *nothing at all* that you *have* to do, much less think about or change or anything else," she was told. With most people the observer fades from the picture afer a few times, but in Hidden's case the observer somehow became *more* active each time, something that we remain perplexed about. I thought about some other client just like her, and I said to that woman, "just go ahead and let that hidden observer exercise itself as much as it can so we can get a better idea of what we're dealing with here," and sure enough, we gained some important information from it.

The next time, she was instructed, "Hidden, as you adjust yourself in that chair, I want you to *listen very carefully* to all the words that follow. Of course, you can recall quite clearly how early on we assured you that there is *nothing* you need to do, *nowhere to be*, no expectations to meet, and no one to please, and if you want,

metaphor

pacing

direct question

pacing

prescribing the symptom

prescribing the symptom

not knowing/not doing

you don't even have to listen to the words, which can tend to *drift in*, or *drift out.*"

"I felt a light trance," she remarked after that session, and her predominant thought, she said, was "*All the things* I have to do later today." "That's very good," I told her. "Aiming for no more than a *very light trance* may be realistic at this juncture."

pacing

restraint

She was provided with customary reassurance and encouragement. and the next time she came in, sat back, closed her eyes, and loosed one deep, refreshing breath, obviously ready to *pay little* heed to that friendly observer. "Hidden," I asked, "I wonder just how deeply into trance you can go today, and as she settled deeper into that chair, I had my answer. Seeing her begin to really drift off for the first time, I knew the observer had to be *watching at a considerable distance*, if at all, and I actually began to feel drowsy myself, as I uttered the following words: 'Someone told me one time that it's all about *absorbing* one's attention. Another said *immersion* is where it's at, and still another said *fixating* or *focusing* are what count, which may be the same thing. Those very people mentioned having their attention *arrested* inwardly, or inward *amusement* occurring involuntarily, as well as an outward *immersion* happening purposely, and I still *become confused* by such mental meanderings.'

suggestion

suggestion

*suggestion covering all
   possibilities*

lead away

"Hidden had to admit experiencing some bewildering but *pleasant sensations* in her hands, as well as elsewhere in that body, though precisely where she could not remem-

suggestion

ber later. I let her know, "Hidden, doing just fine, all those *feelings* and *sensations* that develop on the inside, *putting those aside* for a moment, and noticing the outside, the chair supporting your body, sound of my voice, the fabric beneath your finger tips. . . .

suggestion
lead away

"Now, Hidden, for the next few moments I am going to direct more words at the outside of your body, and while that occurs on the outside, you can let your conscious mind deliberate on them, if you wish, while the deepest and most creative part of you makes something important happen on the inside. Exactly what that is may not become apparent until you close your eyes and relax again *away from here*, maybe in a week or so. . . . "

seeding
posthypnotic
suggestion

So, that was the experience of Hidden, and we know that everyone's experience doing anything is unique, from one time to the next. In your case, (client's name), I know that you can learn something important from your time here today, and the next time you come in, *letting go* and *appreciating* may take on a most curious aspect.

activate seed

Intuition Deepening

You may let your experience further develop as I tell you about Winston. Winston never made a lot of money but he was forever immersed in his job in the university comptroller's office. "What keeps you going?" they asked him. "I'm in tuition," he answered. "Tuition?" they asked. "Yes, in tuition, that's me," he said, "not just at the start of the semester, but all year long." So, he was tagged with the nickname Intuition. "I just know things intuitively," said Winston proudly, adding, "they need to solve a problem and they call in Intuition. Like in a dream during the day, things just come to me." His colleagues found Winston's words puzzling, but they just nodded, as he closed his eyes, drifting off into the deepest of daydreams.

Clinical Comments

Clients sometimes have amnesia for a didactic deepening such as Intuition, even though they may remember the therapy component, say a story, age regression, age progression, or some other technique.

How does this work? I think that the mechanism is similar to the amnesia that occurs during alternating stories. To employ this technique, prepare two stories. The second story contains key suggestions directed at your target. You begin the first story, say, a description of driving down a long, boring road, and leave it at a critical juncture, and immediately launch into the second story, say, "The Little Engine that Could." You complete "Little Engine," return to the first story, and continue it to the end. There is no segue between the stories. People tend to have amnesia for the second story, which is what you want.

NOT KNOWING

One of the most permissive and liberal, but also potent suggestions in hypnosis is not knowing/not doing (Hammond, 1990). This entails telling the client, for example, "There's absolutely nothing at all that you need to know, or do, or think about, or change. There's nowhere to be, no one to please, and no expectations to meet. In fact, you don't even have to listen to the words. . . . " There may be no better way to free up clients to not only respond, but respond in their own way. What can be more empowering than that? I use this induction to "join" with people who have control issues. If they did not respond to another induction, I often use this one the second session.

"Not Knowing" Induction

(Client's name), the story I'm about to read you, *some* have responded in a curious way, *others* have discovered something new, in

suggestion covering all possibilities

their body or mind, and a *few people* came to notice and appreciate something rather intriguing in their experience. You can let that mind of yours sleep now, wondering if you will drift off into a *mild, medium* or *deep* trance.

(seed)

bind of comparable alternatives

"What's your name?" I asked. "*Nonie,*" he answered. "Think of no ankle-no leg-no knee, that's me, Nonie." "Nonie," I said, just sit back and close your eyes if you wish, for the next several minutes I'm going to talk to you about *doing nothing,* that's right, nothing at all."

metaphor

not knowing/not doing

Nonie opened his eyes and remarked, "Last doctor had me lift my hand, imagine myself floating on a cloud, as well as other things, but definitely *not* 'nothing at all.'" "Well, Nonie, this is bound to be a different experience for you today, free of the restraints of doing anything."

"Okay," he said, settling back into the chair and closing his eyes. "Nonie," I said, "*Last person* I had in here, I asked her if, as a background sound she would like music, ocean waves, or some other sound . . . and she put up her hand and said, "Nothing at all, *not even words,*" and she just sat back and let trance develop . . . *silently* . . . *progressively* . . . and, *most deeply* while I was quiet for several minutes.

metaphor

suggestion

Nonie did not respond, and certainly no response was necessary, as I could tell that he was *beginning to experience something.*

suggestion

I remember that day, *my* own legs developed a peculiar heaviness, and maybe even a tingling. *I* caught *myself* drifting off into a private reverie, but knew I had to pay close atten-

metaphor

tion to the subject. That night *I* was very fatigued and slept most deeply indeed.

I gazed again at Nonie, he was unmoving, chin now on his chest. He stirred briefly as my words resumed. "Nonie, this 'nothing at all,' we *do* have a few words that address such nothingness, not a void, but a few words to help you let your experience develop as you continue to do nothing at all. You *don't have to* keep your *suggestion* eyes closed, but may open them any time you wish. And you *don't have to* sit still, as moving around can lead to a shift in perspective. *One* *metaphor* *person* one time moved around every now and then and eventually found that each barely perceptible movement carried him deeper and deeper into a most peaceful trance."

Beginning now, (client's name), you can let your experience develop, in your mind and your body both, and I wonder, just wonder, how deeply your mind can sleep. . . .

Several minutes seemed to pass before I spoke again to Nonie: "Just sitting there like that you need to know that there's absolutely nothing at all that you need to do or know or change. You don't even have to listen to the words, which may drift in or drift out, possibly more out than in, and sometimes a *word* *voice suggestion* that lingers inward can be like a *voice that goes* with you. I know that your unconscious mind is wise and can pick up anything important, even if your conscious mind lets go to the point of disregarding many things spoken here today."

I kept talking to Nonie about voices, and learned later that the words were unremarkable but that either the tempo or the volume later resurfaced now and then at opportune moments of conscious stillness.

I will tell you today, (client's name), just as I told Nonie way back then, "Your experience today is yours and yours alone. There's no where to be, no one to please, and no expectations to meet. You *need not* use this time to enjoy and appreciate the pleasantness and comfort of mild or even moderate relaxation, as to do so could indicate an unexpected depth of experience at unforeseen levels. Some people require a considerable passage of time before they permit themselves to *enter another state*, and we're not talking about moving from Ohio to Louisiana."

restraint

pun
lead away

So, that was the first session with Nonie. By the second visit I was a bit familiar with his response on the inside, and it was not necessary to even mention feelings in his extremities, such as *tingling or numbness, lightness or heaviness*, or *coolness or warmth*, and I simply said to him, "Nonie, those curious sensations *out* there, either *in* your hands or feet, or somewhere else, let them happen now. Not consciously, of course, and not even *automatically, independently*, or *effortlessly*, if you're not ready to do so." "I've been ready for some time and I'm way ahead of you," he whispered.

apposition of opposites

suggestion covering all
  possibilities

(Client's name), those *curious sensations* signal the beginning of trance in most people. They are 'not nothing', and furthermore we know they occur with no conscious effort. Who knows what else can develop, feelings in your *body*, images in your *mind*?

suggestion

apposition of opposites

I will be quiet for a while. You can let your experience develop and I will resume speaking after a few minutes.

Deep Breath Deepening

In a moment I'm going to ask you to take two deep breaths, breathing in, and then breathing out, slowly, as I count from 10 to five during the first exhalation, and from five to one during the second breath out. All you have to do is breathe in and exhale slowly, taking the first breath now, and breathing out as I count, 10 . . . , 9 . . .

Clinical Comments

If people do not respond to such a bombardment of suggestions that say, in effect, "You don't have to do anything at all," then a confusional induction should be considered next.

GOING INSIDE

Most clients readily respond to suggestions for an internal focus. This induction, more than the others, explicitly capitalizes on a person's inclination to focus attention internally.

"Going Inside" Induction

A woman named Chere was good at *daydreaming*. She dwelled on *memories* from the past, or *fantasies* about the future, and she contemplated some things thoroughly, wondered about other things partially, and even immersed her attention completely in one thing to the exclusion of anything occurring on the *inside*, outside, or anywhere else.	*suggestion* *suggestion* *suggestion*

"*A most curious absorption,*" she was prone to say, and until one lazy afternoon I wasn't sure what she meant by this notion of "*a most curious absorption.*" "Give me an example," I told her.

"Well," she said, "You've held an apple, have you not?" "Of course," I answered. She continued, and as she did I became transfixed by her words, as she had a way of speaking—not quite a whisper—that tends to draw a person into her experience. "Massaging a person with her words," I thought at the time.

She said, "One time a friend of mine held up an apple and began to talk about *journeying inside.* My friend, she went by her last name, Inskeep, she said, 'I wonder what's *inside* her . . . ,'and whether she meant inside me or inside the apple, I still don't know to this day."

suggestion

Just then Chere took out an apple and moved it rapidly from her left hand to her right, and my attention was arrested as that apple moved from right hand to left, back and forth, gripping it firmly yet softly, right to left, and her words became distant. I found it easier to just close my eyes, and thinking back now, my own hands began to experience something. "Listen with your *third ear,*" she whispered, "and you know what that means." I nodded my head slowly one more time.

suggestion

I continued listening to her words: "I'm examining this apple very closely, and I take note of the obvious features on the outside, the whisp of a stem that once connected it to the branch, the silkiness of the skin, and yellow blending into the dappled red. Is it a Braeburn apple? A Fuji, or Granny Smith? No, it's just a pedestrian apple, the kind they make cider out of. This apple belongs among those that were undeveloped, a product of a drought or a freeze, or those with a blemish or bruise. Not one of those perfect apples in a gleaming row at the supermarket."

As I listened, I *thought of long ago*, walking through an apple orchard. I was drawn into many pleasant *memories of the past*, and *imaginings of the future*, but I was also drawn to my hands. With the sheer lightness in those hands, how come they were not rising from my lap? "Those hands can take on a life all their own," she said, and a short time later I felt one hand lifting ever so gradually from my lap, while the other hand was *leaden/laden* with a weight. "'Let that heaviness and comfort spread out to the rest of you,' that's what Inskeep told me once," said Chere. "I also recall her saying, 'Isn't it nice to know that you can share this pleasantness and well-being with your mind and body both?'"

I nodded my head again. My mind drifted to bobbing for apples in grade school during Halloween, and my mouth had a peculiar dryness. "Wouldn't the bite of any apple just then be most welcome?" I thought.

I heard the apple touch the table just then, as Chere had set it down, and her words continued, in the direction of the apple or me, I was not sure. "Looking at this wonderful fruit, wondering about the inside, I find it most *inciting/inviting*, contemplating what's in cider,

age regression

age progression

misspeak

misspeak

inside of her aside from the outside, in the cidermill, before *there/here/now.* . . . Millicent was her name, and she ran the cider mill, and at one time she thought she was *unavailable/ invisible* on the inside, but right now, regarding this apple, not the peeling, beyond the sweet tartness, the pulp, and seeds, the corner *core/store* is a good place to shop for daily necessities, is it not? Wasn't it Colin Wilson who first wrote about 'the outsider'?"

confusion

misspeak

misspeak

My legs felt as though they belonged to another, my body became part of the chair, while my mind had journeyed far, far away, distant, but most enjoyably so. Chere's last words had been most curious, and I suddenly experienced what she meant by "a most curious absorption," but I try and retrieve those words now and I draw a complete blank.

She was quiet for several seconds, or maybe minutes, I know not. I heard her pick up the apple and set it down again. Perhaps I had dozed off briefly, and then her words resumed: "When Millicent went on vacation, she took a tour inside the Capulin volcano. While inside, a man said to her, 'I'm in stocks and bonds,' and she reflexively answered, "I'm *in cider.*" He asked, "Yes, *inside* her now, inside this volcano, because volcanoes are feminine, like ships?'" She did not answer.

pun
suggestion

"Inside that volcano she *discovered* many things about herself, and after she returned to work in cider, each day produced more than one fertile reflection," Chere said.

suggestion

Following that experience with Chere and the apples, I slept deeply for the longest time.

Pleasant Image Deepening

I would like you to think back on some pleasant experience from the past, any time, anywhere, whatever comes to mind, some experience inside or outside, when you were alone or with others, just letting that pleasant image fill your mind, as your experience deepens, yes deepens, and I'll resume speaking again in a while.

Clinical Comments

In this induction, the therapist experiences as many hypnotic phenomena as the client. With some clients such modeling may be effective, as it is disarming and unexpected.

With clients who are analytical, I sometimes end this induction with lead away. For example, "Following that experience with Chere, I slept very deeply, and as I slept I dreamed, and in my dream I awoke in class, and there were *three oranges* on the desk."

3

Inductions for Sleep

We are all affected by the amount and quality of sleep we obtain. Sleep has broad, systemic effects on mood, performance, and physical functioning (Bootzin et al, 2003). Insomnia is the experience of inadequate, insufficient, or nonrestorative sleep, despite ample time in bed (Drake, Roehrs, & Roth, 2003). As many as 32.2% of the U.S. population experience insomnia (Ohayon, 2002), and insomniacs typically complain of poor sleep due to unwanted thoughts, worries, and concerns (Harvey & Payne, 2002).

Psychological treatment of insomnia has yielded various degrees of success. These strategies include thought suppression (Salkovskis & Campbell, 1994); solving mental arithmetic problems (Haynes, Adams & Franzen, 1981); distraction with imagery (Harvey & Payne, 2002); and related approaches. In Becker's (1994) study involving two sessions of hypnosis, he found that long-term improvement was predicted by no history of major depression and lack of secondary gain.

These inductions incorporate sleep research findings in two ways: (1) the suggestion of heaviness models slow-wave sleep, the deepest level of sleep, and (2) the suggestion of ideosensory phenomena in the extremities correlates with warmth in hands and feet, which precedes sleep in many subjects. Dreaming in many subjects is up and down in terms of frequency and affect intensity, and dreaming EEG is very similar to awake EEG. This means that dreaming is *not relaxing* (Haynes, personal communication, 2005); however, mention of rapid eye movement and dreaming in an induction does not appear to detract from relaxation and improved sleep in most clients.

In my practice, people who are referred for insomnia are typically on antidepressants, anxiolytics, mood stabilizers, and other agents that may promote sleep. Many of these clients have already tried lifestyle changes and "sleep hygiene" techniques, such as avoiding caffeine, using bed only for sex or sleep, or CBT techniques such as keeping a "worry log." These clients often have tried hard to sleep and of course, this is like trying hard to rid oneself of anxiety, it only serves to worsen and prolong the problem. The suggestions embedded in the following inductions were designed to distract from such conscious effort and to achieve a letting go, which for some clients is a novel idea.

SOUND SLEEP

In my practice I typically see clients with insomnia for two to five sessions, and then make them an audiotape for continued practice. In the first session I usually test response by employing a story induction, counting-down deepening, and the "Three Lessons" story (Gafner & Benson, 2000; Wallas, 1985), the metamessage of which is that clients have resources within themselves to help solve their problems. During the second session I frequently use one of these sleep inductions. If in the initial session the person responds with no hypnotic phenomena (e.g., "I really didn't feel anything"), I may reach for a confusional induction, such as "Seeing the Colors," or the

"Mystifying" induction (Gafner & Benson, 2000). Clients who need to be fortified with ego strengthening may typically receive metaphorical ego strengthening with a sleep induction for a couple of sessions before receiving a sleep induction. The sleep induction that elicits the best response is what I put on the audiotape. I always build in an anchor during the first session and encourage "relaxation practice" at home. I have found that of clients who continue to use the anchor and tape, 60 to 70% maintain at least moderate relief from insomnia.

Notice that the following inductions are all-inclusive in that an additional therapy component is not required. That doesn't mean that additional stories or anecdotes *can't* be used, only that they usually are not necessary.

Sound Sleep Induction

Everyone knows how pleasant it can be to get a good night's sleep, and even a *nap* during the day can be quite refreshing *Waking up*,   *truisms*
arising from bed, and getting ready to go about our day, sometimes we *contemplate* our dreams the night before. We *may have* a vivid   *truisms*
recollection of a dream, or only a fragment of it may remain in our memory. Some people report the *same dream*, or a version of it, one night and then another, and some even *experience* a continuing dream, a most *curious* phe-   *hypnotic language*
nomenon.

Beginning now, I would like you to let yourself *drift off* and dream in your own way, let-   *suggestions*
ting yourself *experience* a deep and comfortable level of relaxation, as I describe to you the work of a pioneering project on lucid dreaming, the kind of dreaming that involves the ability to think about—and even deliberately   *implication*
transform a dream—during the dream.

I wonder *when* you will begin to notice, just

notice, those familiar sensations in your body, usually in *those* extremities, maybe a tingling or numbness or some other feeling, and a nice *comfortable breath* can follow, *independently*, *all by itself*, with *no conscious effort* then you can let yourself go even more.

dissociative language

contingent suggestion
bind of comparable
*   alternatives*

Perhaps you can recall some time in the past when you slept ever so comfortably and pleasantly, when your body *barely moved* if at all, and involuntary process reigned supreme, your breathing regular and even, and if you dreamed, those eyes moved, all by themselves, in sustained bursts, about one per second during the dream.

catalepsy

In the Lavender Sleep Laboratory, subjects were instructed, before going to sleep, to signal when they heard a description of a nature scene. "When you hear it you may signal by one of two ways," they were told, "with a deep breath, or by moving your eyes back and forth from side to side."

A woman named Panamint was subject number one. She had been up late the night before and had no trouble drifting off to sleep. Her observer had some difficulty keeping her own eyes open and may have even dozed off briefly. After what *seemed like several hours*, but in fact was just three, the observer discerned robust eye movements. She looked down at her script and read the following to Panamint: "We deeply appreciate the mysterious aspects of living nature."

time distortion

Panamint signaled with her eyes, and later, when she awoke, refreshed and reinvigorated, she *remembered very little* of her dreaming

amnesia

experience, except that in the dream, she
moved her body with *great effort.*   *catalepsy*

The second subject, Griswold, had reluctantly enrolled in the project, and his ruminations served to keep him awake most of the
night. He had *ignored* the instruction booklet   *discharging resistance*
and instead of just letting it happen, he con-
sciously willed himself to sleep. Griswold's
observer was poised with his script, awaiting
those familiar bursts of eye movements,
which never came, and after four hours he
also did what he was told *not* to do, and   *discharging resistance*
became immersed in the subject's tossing and
turning, and then his own eyes closed, and he
became the dreamer himself, lost in a sweet
oblivion that he *could not recall* once he awoke   *amnesia*
with sunrise.

The third subject, Greensleeves, thought
back on his sleep the night before, when his
body was so heavy and he spontaneously *let go*   *suggestion*
and drifted and dreamed. This was not
Greensleeves's first visit to the sleep labora-
tory, and he recalled his observer's words
another time: "Greensleeves, you don't have to
wait to experience those *weights* on your   *catalepsy*
body." Ever after, when he went to bed at
night, Greensleeves told himself, "You don't
have to wait for the weights," very comforting
words indeed. Another observer had said
something highly curious to him another
time, the words being, "Greensleeves, you
don't need a *translator* to have a *trance later,*"   *pun*
and those words played in his mind now. He
could recall how, in his younger days, he had
slept in a little house by the railroad tracks,

and he *did not hear* the frequent passing of freight trains, which only served to deepen his experience.

negative hallucination

He drifted off to sleep now, and after 60 minutes the observer noted his eyes move, and he began to read from his script: "In the sunset she saw beauty and stillness in the fields of snow."

The subject responded first with his eyes, and then the observer continued to read: "I remember the quiet, the shimmering silence of the pond." Greensleeves responded with *a deep breath*, and his eyes showed that he continued to dream. The observer's words were heard again: "We drifted among the cattails and ferns, slowly drifting downstream."

suggestion

This time the subject's right index finger twitched and moved ever so slowly up into the air, something the observer had never seen in all his years at the laboratory. Just then the subject's lips moved, but the observer could not make out the words.

Greensleeves rolled on his back and *slept* even more deeply and peacefully, dreaming dreams only known to the deepest part of himself. The observer, having done his job, closed his own eyes and became *absorbed* in a most enjoyable reverie.

suggestion

suggestion

Staircase Deepening

I'm going to count slowly, down from 10 to 1, and as those numbers descend, I'd like you to imagine yourself going down a staircase, elevator, or escalator, just letting yourself go deeper with each number counted down. 10 . . . , 9 . . .

BOREDOM

In the following induction, only suggestions aimed at key phenomena, and misspeak, are highlighted. These are opportunities for the reader to employ a subtle vocal shift.

Boredom Induction

Had I needed to count sheep to *fall asleep* during my long train ride across Australia, there was plenty of opportunity to count the myriad wooly creatures, and of course, there was always the splendid landscape to get *lost in*. It was midday, I was gazing idly out the window, and I was about to enter a *state of slumber* when a man moved into the seat next to me.

"Don't doze off just yet," he said. I was taken aback by this intrusion, and just then he continued, "I am Paul Bland and I have a reputation for being terribly *boring*. In school they called me Pall Bland, P-a-l-l, as if I was some tedious entity, and some people would actually fall asleep in my presence." I regarded this man. His face was lined with weariness and there was nothing outstanding about his features. He was remarkable for his lack of individuality. The words *studied anonymity* came to mind and just then he said, "Highly quotidian am I."

"Most curious," I commented, as I stifled a yawn, which in turn produced a yawn from him. Bland went on, in an expressionless tone on some colorless topic. Was it the odor of mothballs I smelled emanating from his apparel? It couldn't be coming from his polyster suit.

"What's your name again?" he asked. "Melody, call me Melody," I answered. "Well, Melody," he said, "Some people think that staring at a fish tank for hours is *boring*, but listening to me may produce sleep, and you might mentally *drift off*, or you could *lose yourself* in the blather of my words, and if any of those things happen, I won't take it personally."

His words were already drifting in and out of my consciousness, though not in a pleasant way, like when you become absorbed in music or a good book. Instead, I recalled a boring lecture in school, the Weather channel, standing in a long line at the store, interminable delays in traffic, or waiting for a long-winded person to get to the point, . . . waiting, waiting. . . .

I must have *dozed off* to sleep, because when he stopped talking a rather loud silence ensued, causing me to snap to attention. I looked at him and there he sat, mouth agape, eyes closed. I regarded Bland very closely, and aside from his strange clothing, he had no outstanding features and would definitely blend into any crowd.

I turned my attention again to the sheep outside the window, miles and miles of sheep. I leaned back, closed my eyes, and I remember my body feeling very, very heavy, but my mind was light, if you can imagine such a thing, and in my reverie I was buoyant, floating on airy gossamer, perhaps on a sunbeam, and I rose, up on high, and found myself in the loftiness of a cloud, or was it on a mountaintop? My memory of the experience is hazy now, but I *do* recall the awareness of *sensation*, my mind being at the promontory of feeling or expression, along with a clarity of understanding, all of which was contrasted with my very *leaden body*. Oh, a heady elixir it was, a most invigorating immersion!

A buzzing drone penetrated my musing, and I realized that Bland had resumed speaking. "But let me tell you about a person even more boring than I," he intoned. "I had a business one time in Omaha, a clock store, Bland's Clocks it was called. It was just after lunch and I was about to take a brief nap. Amidst the soft elevator music I heard the chime of the door opening and a woman came in. She looked prim and proper, about 65 or so, rather wealthy in her beige suit and diamonds. It had been a *slow* week and even slower day and I immediately thought, 'She's here to buy a grandfather clock, or maybe an expensive watch.' However, I was in for a big *surprise*.

"She said in a husky tone, 'Good day, sir,' and proceeded to pick among the cheap novelty items by the check-out. I watched her for what *seemed an eternity*, and finally she clasped a $1.99 sand dial and held out a five-dollar bill. As I reached for the money, she gently pulled it back and said, 'First, you must know who I am.' She set down the sand dial, the sand drizzling down, and proffered a sheaf of papers. I took the papers. That hand with the $5.00 bill remained extended, as her gaze bore into my own hands, which were now turning the first page, the second, the third. . . .

"Eventually I reached page 50 or so. I looked at both sides of every page, and each was blank. Nothing, totally blank, except the last page. She remarked, 'See that?!' It was a mark or smudge on the last page. I didn't answer her, as I had become transfixed by this whole curious matter. 'You can become *totally absorbed* in that very spot,' she said softly, 'and before one minute passes you will realize something of great consequence.'

"I studied that spot for maybe three of four minutes, occasionally glancing up at the woman, whose eyes remained riveted to the spot. The elevator music in the background was suddenly prominent, but then I tuned it out, and redoubled my efforts to discern something of importance from that spot. My body—especially my feet—became *very heavy*, and I pulled up a chair and sat down, never allowing my eyes to leave that spot.

"At some point my eyes closed and inside I began to experience that curious sense of levity, while my body melded further into the chair. So *dense and weighty* was my body that I could not move a muscle. The sheer heaviness of my body increased, while once again, the lightness of my mind elevated itself to indescribable heights. I remained absorbed in this state for what seemed like hours.

Somewhere in my mind I heard the chime of the door, someone entering or exiting, and then I heard it again. When I opened my eyes, the woman was gone. The pile of papers was still there, along with the five-dollar bill. A young boy stood at the counter. '*When* can I buy this clock, mister?' he asked.

"At the end of the day I returned home, feeling both exhilarated and exhausted. As I lay down in bed that night I pulled up the covers, closed my eyes, and began what turned out to be a most profound and restful sleep."

Sand Dial Deepening

That's the way, (client's name), doing just fine. Beginning now I would like you to picture in your mind a sand dial, any kind you wish, grains of sand *releasing* themselves, a trickle of sand, slow and steady, but much too fast to count the grains. Just watch that sand dial in your mind, and when the top portion has emptied completely, you and I will know that you are sufficiently deep in order to proceed, and you will find your head nodding two times. Just taking as much time as you need, that's right. . . . "

SLUMBER PILL

I have found this induction to be remarkably effective. Whether people respond because of the induction's directness or brevity, I do not know. I do know that many of my clients are on medications, have had their insomnia treated with medications, and may be oriented, as many in society are, to the notion that taking a pill is the answer to many problems. Asking a client to imagine taking a "slumber pill" may indeed join with this mindset.

Slumber Pill Induction

I would like you to imagine yourself in bed, preparing for a *good night's sleep*. You place a pill in your mouth. It is a small tablet, lavender in color, oval shaped, and about the size of a baby aspirin. You swallow it now. It goes down easily, that imaginary pill descending into you. That's the way. It is entering your system now, *silently, swiftly*, and *most effectively*.

Your eyes close all by themselves and you adjust yourself in a comfortable position, preparing yourself for the rapidly dissolving portion of this slumber pill, which begins to work almost immediately, promoting a *nice, sound sleep* in a few minutes. The remaining portion of this pill dissolves more slowly, helping you sustain your sleep during the rest of the night. However, you may just forget about how this pill works, as I direct some words to the front part of your mind.

One time I saw a woman named Amber, who sought assistance for insomnia. She had some discomfort in her body, but she also had a very busy mind. "It's like a tape recorder that doesn't shut off," were her words. I carefully instructed Amber, "Let's *slow down* that chatter in your mind. You still hear the words, but they are becoming garbled, barely audible, as I direct some words to your body, yes that body, which already is becoming quite *heavy*. As you lie there still, like a placid pool of water with very few ripples, and those overhanging trees near the pool, can you hear the silence between the leaves?

"Amber, as you breathe in and breathe out, you exhale any worry or negativity. Can you still hear that self-talk, or is it even more distant than it was before? I would like you to imagine now, just imagine, a feeling of *comfort* up there at the top of your head, and I don't know if it is a feeling of coolness or warmth, or some other pleasant feeling. That comfortable feeling begins to descend now, down your face, down your neck, continuing downward, and each part of your body that it touches, you sink *deeper and deeper* into a *profound* sense of pleasantness and comfort.

I don't know how long it will take for this comfort to extend down to the tips of your toes, but just let that feeling continue now. Deeper and deeper into a most pleasant experience of *comfort and relaxation*.

I told another person who took the slumber pill, "Let that mind sleep now, just sleep ever so deeply. Don't you deserve a nice, restful sleep? Of course you do! If you need to arise during the night to attend to nature's call, I know and you know that you can resume your sleep. Just let that pill do its job, all by itself, independently, automatically, involuntarily and *unconsciously*."

Sleep for him was now very near and more words were hardly necessary. However, I told him the following:

Estate Sale Deepening

You may let your experience develop and deepen as I tell you about last weekend when I started out on a drive around town. The first sign I came to said "Yard Sale." I slowed down but did not stop and then I drove on. The next sign I came to said "Garage Sale," and I continued on. After a while I encountered another sign that said "Patio Sale," and I drove on. The next sign said "Rummage Sale" but I continued down the road. It seemed like a long time had passed, and eventually I came to another sign that said "Estate Sale." I stopped, sat back in the seat, closed my eyes, took one deep, refreshing breath, and drifted off into another state.

RUMINATION

Even more than chronic pain, unwanted thoughts are the number one reason clients in my practice have trouble falling asleep or staying asleep. In our busy world, with so many worries and responsibilities, it is a tall order to switch off or shut out unwanted thoughts. With many other things in life we simpy flip a switch or click a mouse and the job is done; however, not so with ruminations by day, or especially ruminations by night. This induction is designed to directly counteract the behavior of the excessive ruminator.

Rumination Induction

In a moment I'm going to count slowly from 25 to 1, just like this, "25 . . . , 24 . . . ," and while you hear those numbers descending down, I would like you to imagine your relaxation deepening, *ever so gradually*. I remember one person one time, he told me later that as he listened to the numbers going *down*, he imagined a comfortable warmth going all *down* his body. Another person said that as she heard the numbers she had an image of soothing coolness beginning at her feet and going *up* her body, just a bit at a time.

25 . . . , 24 . . . (continuing to count slowly to 1).

When Dee was a kid she was fascinated by her mother's big jewelry box that had multiple tiers with drawers and small box sections on the top. There was a place to hang necklaces in a door that swung out. Each small box held one pair of earrings while the stacked drawers held larger items such as bracelets or watches. *Each piece of jewelry had a specific place to rest.* Dee never ceased to marvel at the detail and organization of the box. "Everything had its place," she recalled.

Her brother, Sloan, an avid fisherman, had a tackle box that served a similar purpose, and even though he thought everything had its place, Dee knew that in her mother's jewelry box everything was *just right.*

Let your mind *sleep* now. Sleep very deeply, as there's nothing you need to know or do or think about. This is your time to enjoy and appreciate the *pleasantness and comfort* of deep relaxation.

Everyone talks during the day, and sometimes we even talk to ourselves, in our minds, mulling over this or that. This serves a useful purpose when we're awake, but you *don't need* that self-talk at night when you're going to sleep. Don't you deserve a pleasant and relaxing sleep?

Some people call it a garage sale, others call it patio sale, rummage sale, or any variety of names, but you know what I mean. Many people may bring a large assortment of goods together and arrange them in orderly fashion, men's clothing here, women's over there, furniture here, stuffed animals over there. Perhaps color coded label designate who owns what, blue dots were put on by the Jones, orange by the Garcias, and the *Dozers*, who knows what color they had?

You can take any random thoughts that drift through your mind, consolidating them into just one space. As they are placed in their compartment they can dissipate from your mind, as quickly as predicted rainfall that never really happened. You can enjoy a nice, deep refreshing breath and *let that mind clear*. Sleeping deeply now, but *sleeping* even deeper at home.

One person one time, I forget her name, she quickly mastered the technique of compartmentalization by lying down at night and imagining her thoughts flying into a small drawer. The very first session she said, "I'm looking forward to the time when I can look back," and from right then she began to appreciate a really *good night's sleep*. Another person, who also achieved a pleasant night's sleep, he said, "I don't mind storing my evening thoughts away, but I choose to compartmentalize only 80% of them." He had a good reason for doing so, but I forget what it was. That same man said, "Once I let go and slept, checking the perimeter wasn't necessary, as I realized it would still be there in the morning."

I can remember when someone would read me bedtime stories, preparing me for a nice, restful sleep. You may recall such a story now, or maybe all you can think about is Dee and her jewelry box. It really doesn't matter at all. Beginning now, (client's name), I would like you to slowly move that right hand, letting your thumb and first finger come together, forming a little circle. This anchor, or reminder, is your connection between here and home, as it can trigger *slowing down* and *heaviness* in your body, and doing what you need to with random thoughts, as you prepare to sleep. You may wish to combine your anchor with one deep, refreshing breath. That's the way. . . .

Double Deepening

Allow your experience to deepen as I count from 10 to 1 now, 10, 9, 8, 7, 6, 5, 4, 3, 2, 1 . . . *and* back up to five and down again, 5, 4, 3, 2, and 1.

WALKING THROUGH TIME

Many of us are familiar with the pleasant fatigue that results from a walk in the outdoors. This induction emphasizes catalepsy and anesthesia (hypnotic phenomena that may precede sleep), along with suggestions for tiredness, slowing down, and sleep itself. As clients understand the reason for their visit (insomnia), they tend to especially self-reference the suggestions for sleep.

Walking Through Time Induction

Stephens and Staves did many things together, pleasant, leisurely things, and looking back, years later, their fond recollections produced a most *enjoyable reverie*, something they could become absorbed in for a portion of the day or night, for many minutes or hours, or just for timeless moments whenever they chose.

Their present venture was very special, as well as arduous and uncertain, as they literally were about to walk through time. Yes, they were to traverse the length of the Grand Canyon, a vast, cleaving space that is a mile deep at its center, 200 river miles long, and averages 10 miles across. Most of its 1,000 square miles had never experienced human footfall, not until Staves and Stephens began to traverse the canyon on May 8, 1962.

Stephens and Staves gazed out upon the canyon and contemplated their journey. They had arranged for drops of supplies at key locations, and they had prepared physically and mentally for the journey. But they forgot about all those things amidst the vast silence of the early morning. The quiet was suddenly penetrated by the cawing of a crow, a seeming sacrilege of this revered time and space. "You want to walk the length of this?" asked Staves. Stephens waited three long seconds before answering: "Come along and see what you may *discover*."

They started down the trail, Staves following reluctantly, as her companion spoke to no one in particular: "We think we know what's down there." "We don't know what we don't know," offered Staves. Stephens continued: "Bobcats, wild horses, bighorn sheep, insects, single algae. What I want to get lost in are the rocks, the ever changing colors, and experience how time has carved those rocks." "The impenetrable silence, I've always wondered about that," commented Staves. Stephens was now several paces ahead, and she did not hear the words.

They trudged on. "It *lightens* my heart to go *deep*," uttered Stephens. "What did you say?" asked Staves, her body growing *heavier* with each step. "In here, miles become meaningless," thought Staves to herself. Her footfalls touched prints of horses' hooves. "There's a legend about the little horses of the Esplanade, miniature horses of the Canyon," said Stephens over her shoulder.

Near nightfall they approached Hualapai canyon. The sandstone platform took on the blue-gray softness of the evening. "My legs feel as though they belong to another," said Staves. They set up camp and had a fire going in no time. After eating, they climbed into their sleeping bags, as they were so very, *very tired*. Their eyes gazed at the camp fire with heavy eyes, as sleep was near. Their focus was both concentrated and diffuse, a communion with the natural world beyond the fire.

"My body is down here but my mind is still out there, above the canyon," whispered Stephens. Staves recalled the words she had read in *Millenium Archives* . . . "no cataclysm created the Canyon. Instead, some 7 million years ago the Colorado River had meandered lazily across a plain. A massive dome pushed up in the river's path, and the dome rose, an inch every hundred years or so, and the river cut through the dome, slowly forming the canyon."

Long moments passed and Staves said, "Tell me again about that medicine woman you went to last year." Nearly a full minute passed before Stephens answered: "I went there for help solving a problem, but I ended up learning a lot about my body. She taught me hypnoanesthsia and hypnoanalgesia, and I still don't know the difference between the two. She said to me, 'You may remember when you were young, playing in the snow so long that your hands became *cold and numb* . . . ,' and you can imagine how my hands started to feel; however, both my feet became even *more* numb, and they actually felt quite *separated* from the rest of me."

"Highly strange," commented Staves. Stephens continued: "I still use that numbness in different ways. It used to be that whenever I was touched on the neck or back it tickled terribly, but now whenever I'm touched there,

I tell myself, 'Take over, numbness,' and any touch actually feels quite good. "I remain a skeptic of such things," said Staves.

Stephens went on: "I used to be afraid of heights, but now when I'm up high I say the same thing to myself and I immediately become 'insensitive' to my nervousness. The medicine woman told me one time after her favorite horse passed away her *inner analgesia* became an agent like Maalox that coated her heart with soothing protection." Staves' eyes had now closed and she was fast asleep, and soon her partner followed.

In the days ahead they stopped by a narrow hanging terrace below Great Thumb Point. The sun on their backs was a sharp contrast to the raw wind of the early morning. Stephens grasped a small stick and kneeled down on the trail. The stick in her hand moved *automatically* as she drew an animal figure in the sand. Staves stared at the drawing for the longest time, and then she saw only sand, no hand with stick, no animal figure, no Stephens. "Without even trying you cannot feel the warm sun on your skin," said Staves.

Stephens responded, "I can hear Medicine Woman's voice right now." They continued down the trail the next day, and the days led to weeks. Their minds carried them to experiences in the past, and they imagined themselves in the future, experiencing a host of things in body and mind, and every night, they *slept ever so deeply* by the camp fire (Fletcher, 1966).

Navajo Weavers Deepening

You may let your experience deepen as I tell you about Navajo weavers. When they plan a new rug, Navajo weavers have many decisions to make: selecting the theme, proper colors, and everything else that goes into the project, which may take many months to complete. Sometimes they consult a grandmother from generations past to help in the decisions. Collective archived family experience nothwithstanding, such a search, or consultation, may be viewed as seeking direction from the unconscious mind. Beginning now, I would like you to consult the back part of your mind to help your experience deepen. Let your mind drift and dream and when you are sufficiently deep, you will know and I will know because you'll find yourself taking one deep, satisfying breath.

DECLINE OF CORAL REEFS

In my first session with a client I speak about the difference between an indirective and directive approach in hypnosis. This introduction includes examples of metaphor and embedded suggestion (e.g., "If you say 'My plate is full' or 'I have to shoulder a heavy load,' you're speaking metaphorically.") So, too, if I tell a client a story about someone else slowing down while driving their car, that *slowing down* is an example of how we embed suggestions, something known to help people with their problem. Accordingly, the client is not only informed about the approach to hypnosis that will be used, which is framed as helping, but important suggestions are seeded ahead of time. At that early juncture I don't know which induction I will be using, but I do know that the client is prepared to self-reference suggestions such as those offered in the Decline of Coral Reefs induction.

Decline of Coral Reefs Induction

You know how it is when we speak of one thing in terms of another. For example, the following hypnotic induction has to do with sleep, *nice, sound sleep*, but what I'm about to read to you describes something else, coral reefs in the ocean. Just sit back now and close your eyes as I tell you something you may not have realized about coral reefs.

One time not long ago a good friend gave me very precise instructions. She said, "Attend this lecture—here is the time and place on this paper—and pay very close attention, and even take notes if you need to."

"Why?" I asked. "Because a portion of this lecture will directly apply to you and may provide you with some answers at this time in your life," she said. "I'll do it," I responded, as I didn't have anything better to do that day. The lecture took place several days in the future, but it seemed like only a few moments passed before I found myself in the crowded lecture hall at the university. It was very quiet in there considering the throng of people, and I *dozed off*, only to be awakened some time later by the professor's words penetrating my consciousness.

"It may be seen as a *cryptic* loss of coral reef resilience, both in the Pacific and the Caribbean regions," he intoned. The word *cryptic* had seized my attention and I felt a sensory overload that *deadened my body*, a response familiar to me my whole life.

The rest of the words drifted in and out like waves rushing up and back on a shore, and the professor's remaining words were lost on me, and thankfully a transcript, available later on the class website, helped me reconstruct what turned out to be a most *curious experience.*

"Overharvesting, pollution, disease, and climate change are quite evident," continued the professor, "and even the Great Barrier Reef has shown a systematic decline." "*Cryptic*," I thought again. "Why cryptic?"

"The resilience of reef ecosystems needs to be more actively managed," he said, "and sea urchins . . . " His voice trailed off in my reverie. My conscious mind returned to that word *cryptic*. Its grip on my mind was vise-like. Why *cryptic* loss? The words reverberated, their din blotting out the past, the future, my body, and those around me. I closed my eyes tightly and the sound diminished, and once again I was aware of my legs on the floor, and my arms dangling from my shoulders, though I regarded them as the appendages of another.

Applause from the audience erupted and I awoke with a start. The light dimmed and then the room went totally dark. Was I the only one who noticed? The professor's words continued, but in incomplete sentences, words and phrases pulsating, seeming to bolt me to my chair—". . . coral disease . . . coral bleaching . . . reduced fish stocks . . . terrestrial runoff . . . crown-of-thorns starfish." They jolted my mind and once again the overload led me into the sweet oblivion of dreaming and drifting, as my mind, if not my body, was transported to another place and time. My chin descended to my chest and I slept deeply . . . until once again that word *cryptic* seized my mind.

The words from the podium emanated down to me again— ". . . scraping herbivores . . . grazing parrotfish . . . Galapagos Islands . . . 'no-take' areas where human activities are prohibited . . . pathogens and introduced species . . . " I thought, *"no-take" area*, a highly unusual term, and then once again that word, there it was in my head.

He continued speaking up there, but now it seemed like miles away. I said something to the person next to me, but it came out as a croak in a very small voice. I drew my knees up to my chest and made myself small.

I *drifted off* once again. When I awoke no one was there, but the lights were on. I walked home very slowly, as I was *exhausted* by the day's experience. That night I longed for sleep. I climbed into bed, closed my eyes, and very soon I was *sleeping very deeply* (Bellwood, Hughes, Folke, & Nystrom, 2004).

Nurnt Borton Deepening

Nurnt Borton let his experience deepen as he contemplated the following: Time has passed, time was present, always presenting us with time future. Are they all contained in time past, present, and future? Speculating on futures if all present is eternal time, and time deposits, is any time redeemable? What might have been can be an abstraction, remaining a continuing and perpetual possibility. The present points to one end, now, the end of what might have been and what has been. Big Ben in London chimes on the hour, while in Texas, in Big Bend Park, the experience is timeless (Eliot, 1971).

FOREST OF STONE

One of the most effective techniques I have discovered for working with chronic pain involves an unconsciously directed task. I tell the client, for example, "Beginning now, I would like to assign a task for your unconscious mind. That task is full and complete *relaxation and comfort* all through your body, *slowing down* both your mind and your body. Let your unconscious mind do that now, while I direct some words at the front part of your mind." I then tell the client a story, for example, an ego strengthening story, and build in an anchor at the end of the procedure.

Accordingly, pain control is accomplished and the therapist does very little, as the unconscious mind fulfills the task. The same can be done with insomnia. I customarily say, "Sleep—good, sound sleep—can be achieved by your unconscious mind. You can wall off any unnecessary thoughts, saving them for your waking hours, and full comfort and relaxation in both your mind and your body can be accomplished by your unconscious mind. You can get to sleep promptly, stay asleep, and if you wake up for some reason during the night, or early in the morning, you can return to sleep.

Assign this job of *sound sleep* now, to your unconscious mind, while I direct the following story to the front part of your mind.

Forest of Stone Induction

In 1978 they closed an office of the U.S. Geological Survey in a large city in the western United States. Without celebration or fanfare, the operation moved to new quarters elsewhere, and the old building was demolished. In six months a shopping center was built on the site.

Some of the furniture and office equipment was moved, but most of it was sent away for government auction. John Nesbitt from Carlsbad, New Mexico, attended one of those auctions, and among his inexpensive purchases was a gray, three-drawer filing cabinet. He inspected it when he got home and found that each drawer was empty. John's mind was preoccupied by certain losses in his life, and he just left the filing cabinet in his backyard, returning to his ruminations of regret and solitude. Several weeks later, he did not know why, but for some reason he felt beneath the bottom drawer of the cabinet, and there he discovered a yellowed manila envelope taped to the bottom of the drawer. Inside he found a typewritten report dated November 14, 1951.

The document was addressed to the superintendent of the Petrified National Forest in Arizona. He hurried to the last page and saw that the author's name was blacked out. Nervously shuffling the pages he returned to the beginning, and began to read from the report:

> As you know, President Theodore Roosevelt created this national monument in 1906, thereby making it illegal to remove even the tiniest sliver of petrified wood, fossil, or archeological relic. In the old days, looting of this national treasure was very commonplace. Persons unknown came at night and hauled out wagonloads of petrified wood, which contains valuable crystals that develop naturally in the cavities of the former trees. Even today the thievery continues, but on a much smaller scale. Some citizens have returned what they stole, and it has been my job for the last 30 years to inventory what people have returned, along with any letters that may have accompanied their packages.

I have traversed this national park every day for many years, even at night, when the wind howls and the coyotes beckon one another. By day I gaze upon this panorama of color and forms, and become immersed in the blue-gray haze of lunar landscapes. I experience a parched throat when ambling about these dry tablelands where no spring flows. Beneath the sand can be found remains of earlier geologic periods, dating back some 200 million years. Being of the Hopi Indian tribe, this park is a hallowed place to me, and I give thanks for each piece of this land that is returned to its rightful place.

The very first letter I catalogued was dated July 6, 1910, from someone called Bessie, and it said, "I first went with my father on horseback to the park in 1886. I expected to see a stone forest that consisted of standing trees, with trunks and branches and even twigs, all petrified in place, not chunks of broken logs. My father dug under one log and found this bone awl and drill, something he kept on our mantle for a number of years, along with a clay bowl he found on another trip. Papa has passed on now, and I am returning the bowl and bone tools, something I could never bring myself to do when he was still alive."

Another letter dated January 7, 1948 arrived with a package that was cash on delivery, and the postage was gladly paid. The package contained several pounds of fossils, a fern leaf, a crayfish, an aquatic spider, and a spikey palm frond, along with other things long since sent away for storage. The letter stated, "My father, a parson, stole these relics one night. He had no regrets, but I have been sorrowful for many years. With the return of these treasures my step is now lighter, and for the first time I look forward to a *good sound sleep* when I climb into bed at night."

Another letter from 1912 was from a man named Marcos. He said, "I first visited the Painted Desert when I mustered out of the Union Army in 1865. I returned many times, and with each trip my sadness mounted. However, I did not stop my plunder. I now return to you this cache of relics, and as I mail this package I know that tonight I will *sleep soundly* for the first time in many years." Marcos's package contained dinosaur fragments, bones, an armor plate, a tusk, a stone knife, and a shell bracelet.

Another letter was from a woman in St. Louis. Her package contained a bird's beak and a large chunk of tree. The letter said, in part, "My father purchased these items from a settler in the late 1800s. As a child I became lost as I gazed at the crystal kaleidoscope within. I also had a large seashell and I was fascinated by the roar of the ocean when I held it to my ear. I feel no compunction to return the shell to the sea, but returning these relics to their rightful place is quite another matter."

John Nesbitt read and re-read the letter late into the night. When he finally climbed into bed, he continued to wonder about the man who wrote the report, but in no time he drifted off to sleep and dreamed about sea shells.

25–1 Deepening

You may let your sleep experience develop as I count from 25 down to one. Beginning to count now, 25 . . . 24 . . .

Clinical Comments

I encourage you to compose your own inductions for clients with insomnia. I tend to rely on material set in the natural world, but that may not be your cup of tea. What is of special interest to you? You may not need to look any further than an activity that stimulates your imagination. Just turn it into a story, pepper it with hypnotic language and key suggestions, and voila, you have something in which clients can absorb their attention.

During any hypnosis session clients may fall asleep. I often tell them things like, "Let your mind sleep deeply." Occasionally they take me at my word, and soon I hear a snore. However, sometimes it is difficult to tell if someone is asleep. If I'm not sure, I ask for a response, a finger signal, a head nod, or a deep breath before proceeding.

It is always sound practice to ask for a contingent suggestion; for example, *when* you can see yourself, in your mind, having a good night's sleep, your "yes" finger will rise." Let's say you don't get a response, or maybe you're not sure if the person responded. After a minute or two it is good to simply move on with what you have planned for the session, as sometimes the person in fact responded but you missed the response. When I debrief clients after realerting, many times they will say things like, "Oh, I thought my finger *did* move up into the air."

When I am treating clients with insomnia and they don't see improved sleep after a few sessions, I often proceed to unconscious questioning, as many times an unconscious issue is holding them back. After setting up finger signals (responses for "yes," "no," and "I don't know/I'm not ready to answer yet"), I ask a series of questions directed at possible underlying issues. If the person has PTSD, I immediately go after guilt; for example, "John, in a few seconds I'm going to ask a question of your unconscious mind, and you may answer with one of your fingers. Does guilt have anything to do with your sleep problem? Taking as much time as you need, you will know and I will know when you respond with one of those fingers."

Let's say you have no inkling of an underlying issue. Then you will want to proceed with more general questions: "John, is there some unconscious reason contributing to your insomnia?" If he responds affirmatively, I will then proceed with more specific questions such as, "Does it have to do with guilt?" or "Does it have to do with something from the past?" Depending on the response, I might then ask for a verbal report, such as, "John, tell me *with your words* what comes to mind now." The verbal response will often be a mere fragment, such as, "My mother . . . ," or "Something long ago . . . " After exhausting this search I will verbally process these data during posttrance discussion, and hope to desensitize and reframe the issue so that therapy can proceed.

Insomnia is essentially like any other symptom in that people are stuck and need to be perturbed. In other words, our job is to "stir the pot" and free clients up to respond differently. Sleep researchers divide insomnia into three stages: (1) sleep-onset insomnia, or difficulty falling asleep; (2) middle insomnia, or difficulty staying asleep; and (3) terminal insomnia, or waking up too early. In treating insomnia, it is sometimes unrealistic to expect improvement in all three stages, and my goal for clients is to aim for improvement in one or two stages.

Often insomnia is caused by an inadequately treated Axis I disorder, especially depression and anxiety. Also, don't forget to examine situational issues, which could be a barking dog, worry about an ill family member, or an insufficiently treated medical problem, such as acid reflux disorder or chronic pain. There might be a simple answer to insomnia and no need for you to delve into pattern interruption and unconscious work.

4

Inductions for Children

GENERAL CONSIDERATIONS

There is a sizable literature on the use of hypnosis with childhood medical and other problems. These applications include such issues as hematology/oncology (Jacobs, Pelier, & Larkin, 1998); wart regression (Felt et al., 1998); and dental phobia, to name but a few. The literature is also replete with case reports and studies citing the use of hypnosis for nail biting, thumb sucking, enuresis, and various other presenting issues (Zahourek, 1985). In this chapter I will cover some useful techniques for inducing trance with this population.

With younger children psychotherapy almost always includes some aspect of play therapy. This could include sand tray, coloring or drawing, or absorption in a fantasy, movie, or some similar means. The touchstone reference in this area is Virginia Axline's *Play Therapy* (1947). I would also recommend the works of Axline's student, Sophie Lovinger, whose *Child Psychotherapy* (1998) is a very good reference.

Just as with adults, it is important to regard hypnosis with children as an adjunct to a larger modality. In my practice at the Department of Veterans Affairs I see many couples and families, and therapy with children is usually an adjunct to family therapy.

NINE-YEAR OLD BOY WITH ENCOPRESIS

Nine-year-old Cesar's "accidents in his pants" were the impetus for family therapy. The boy's parents had consulted a pediatrician who found no medical cause for the problem. Intern Paul Williams gleaned on the first interview that Cesar's problem was not the only one in this family of four. The 30-year-old father, who had been an infantryman in the first Gulf war, had a severe cardiac condition, and his wife had recently lost her job. Cesar's brother, Mario, age 12, was the "perfect child," overly helpful to his family, and he received excellent grades in school.

Paul arranged to see the family for 90-minute sessions. The first 30 minutes were with Cesar, who insisted his brother be there with him. Mario lay on the floor playing a videogame while Cesar sat in the recliner with ocean waves playing on the sound machine. Cesar *loved* Godzilla, so the therapist absorbed Cesar's attention in an image of the creature. Cesar's accidents occurred mostly at night, so "sleep time" was incorporated in the following, which is a portion of the second of two hypnosis sessions with Cesar.

Godzilla Induction

Therapist		Client
" . . . by closing those eyes now you can see Godzilla, moving deeper, out into the ocean . . . *and* perhaps you *are* Godzilla, strong, powerful . . .	*linking word* *suggestion*	*closes eyes, moves arms in swimming motion*

feel that strength . . . Godzilla is *in control* of his own body, and as he goes deeper, out into the ocean, his body becomes loose and floppy, like Jel-Lo or spaghetti

  suggestion

"and Godzilla can just sit back and sleep, as if in a dream, loose and floppy, like *Jel-Lo or spaghetti* and I'll be quiet for a few minutes while Godzilla becomes *even more relaxed*—and more powerful, listening to the ocean waves

  pacing   *sits back in chair*

  repetition

  deepening

        fidgets and squirms

"and Godzilla can do anything he needs to do to feel more comfortable, that's the way . . .

  paces

" . . . and now I'm going to count down from 10 to 1, and Godzilla can become even more relaxed and sleepy while I *count*, 10, 9, 8, 7, 6, 5, 4, 3, 2, and 1, . . .

  deepening   *slumps lower in chair*

"and now, while Godzilla is way out there in the ocean, I wonder when Godzilla will choose to *let go* because we know that Godzilla is the *boss* of his own body . . . and we know that when he has let go, he can return to shore, knowing that whenever he needs to slow down, relax, or if he needs a reminder of his power during sleep time, he can make that *little circle* with his thumb and first finger that I showed you last time . . . and now I'm *going to count* from one up to five, and when my voice reaches three, or

  suggestion

  suggestion

        resumes swimming

  suggestion

        makes anchor

  realerting

four, or five you can wake up feeling
really good like after a nice nap, 1,   *wakes up with a*
2, 3, 4 and 5!"   *broad smile*

During the remainder of the session Cesar and Mario worked with
crayons and coloring books in the waiting room while Paul worked with
their parents on communication, conflict management, and issues of
adjustment. Except for one accident, Cesar's encopresis disappeared during the next three months after Paul saw his parents.

Conclusion of Therapy

Children often respond rapidly, as they seem to be especially "response
attentive," or ready and open to suggestion. Therapists need only discover
the child's favorite image or activity, immerse her attention in it, pace and
lead ongoing behavior, and intersperse suggestions aimed at the desired
target.

Cesar's parents had serious problems, but they were not insurmount-
able. I have had similar situations where "our main problem" was, for
example, the child's enuresis or encopresis, and because one or both parents were drug addicted or personality disordered, the parents failed to
show up for appointments, and accordingly, hypnosis did little good for the
child's problem.

SIBLING RIVALRY

The parents, Paula and David, both intensive care nurses, attended therapy
with their children, Elise, age 5, and her sister, Isabella, 14 months older.
The two children, whose adjustment was otherwise normal, fought inces-
santly, striking or biting one another unprovoked. The parents had had the
children evaluated by their pediatrician as well as two child psychologists.
Various behavioral strategies had failed. Medication had been suggested,
but this option was declined by Paula and David. "We can't take them anywhere together, nor can we leave them alone together," said the parents,

who naturally feared serious injury. A first session with the parents alone ruled out a marital problem.

I asked them to have the children bring their favorite toy to the first session. Isabella hugged Barney and Elise carried a Barbie doll. Observing these happy little girls it was difficult for me to imagine them as assaultive helions. The parents went to the waiting room, but only after I promised to watch them very closely.

A teddy bear awaited them on the coffee table, as my plan was to seed teddy bear for the follow-up session. I asked the girls to draw their family with color crayons and paper. All was serene as each smiled and chortled as they worked. As I was commenting on Elise's picture, her sister arose, quickly walked around the coffee table and punched at Elise's head. It proved to be only a glancing blow, as Elise saw it coming and ducked. Seconds later they were both lost again in their drawing. My plan had been to build rapport with the color crayons at the first session, but I quickly opted for a change in plans, saying, "Let's stop those nice pictures now and play Sleeping Bears. How about that?" Elise clapped her hands with glee, and Isabella was set to disagree, but looked down at her picture instead. "Each of you can play in your own way. Sleeping Bears is lots of fun," I said. They gave their approval to lower the lights and I put ocean waves on the sound machine.

Both lay down, one on the love seat, one on the floor, and they closed their eyes and squirmed as I began the following induction.

Sleeping Bears Induction

"The Bear family lived in the forest. Not just any forest, but a magic forest where wonderful things happen. When you looked up in the trees you could see beautiful birds, red ones, yellow ones, and blue ones. What color birds do you see?"

"Green ones, parrots," responded Isabella. "Green ones and purple ones," said Elise. "Monkeys, too," said Isabella. "Very good. Isn't it lots of fun to look at everything up there in those trees?" I asked. They continued to squirm as I went on with the induction.

"There were many other houses with bear families. Some had grandma bear and cousin bear, but our bear family had four bears, mama bear, papa bear, and two little girl bears, Alice and Isabelle." "Do bears really live in a house?" asked Isabella. "These bears do," I answered. Elise opened her eyes and snarled at her sister, "These bears live in *houses*."

I asked them to close their eyes again and listen to the sound of the waves as I continued:

"It was now nighttime and the bears listened to the waves lapping up on the beach not far away . . . and everyone in the bear house was fast asleep. The bear family always fell asleep very quickly, that's why they were called the *Sleeping* Bears. You, too, can dream now, fast asleep, *dreaming and dreaming*."

Balloons Story II Deepening

Betty Bear held her hand tightly to the strings in her right paw. Attached to each string was a balloon. Betty looked up at all the balloons. There were white ones, red ones, green ones, many different colors. She clutched the strings for all those balloons in her right paw.

Betty was at the school carnival with all the other bear children. Her job was to walk around and sell those balloons. "Don't come back until you sell every one," her father had told her. She listened to the music and enjoyed the smell of cotton candy. Everyone else at the carnival was having a fun time, but not Betty.

Two hours passed and Betty had sold only three balloons. "I have 27 more balloons, I'll never sell them all," she thought. Her paw hurt and was sweaty from holding onto all those balloons. A gust of wind came up and blew hard at Betty and her balloons. One balloon escaped her grasp, and she watched it fly up in the air and disappear into the night.

Just then Betty let go another balloon, a red one. Then she let go of two more. She took a deep breath and all the rest of the balloons, she *just let them go.*

Both girls pretended to sleep; the ocean waves continued, and I collected my thoughts.

"What a good job you both did here today playing Sleeping Bears, and the next time you return you can play this game again. I'm going to count from one up to five and by the time I reach five you can wake up feeling really good, 1, 2 . . ."

I escorted them to their parents in the waiting room. "Well, are they cured?" asked Paula. "We're getting there," I said. We made an appointment for next week and the parents took the girls to McDonald's for dinner. I called Paula during the week and asked about feelings that had been elicited in sessions with other therapists. "The gamut, you name it: anger, jealousy, hatred, even wishing death on each other," she said, and then added that the day before Isabella had held her sister's head under water in the pool, and then Elise bit her on the cheek. "You'll see the teeth marks," she added. I told her that I've known plenty of similar siblings who had grown up to become very close as adults.

BEARS SLEEP AGAIN

I audiotaped the next session, which included a retelling of Sleeping Bears and Balloons Story II Deepening, and added dialogue among the Bear family, with the bear parents telling their daughters, Alice and Isabelle, "We love you very much and need everyone to do their best so we can have a happy family." The parents agreed to play the tape to them three times a week before bedtime. I reminded them to maintain safety precautions and to reinforce any behavior that was not fighting.

CHANGE IS HAPPENING: PANDORA'S BOX

David called three weeks later. The girls' fighting had diminished by 50%. I saw them a week after Paul's phone call and with the girls I reviewed the "feeling cards," laminated cards with faces showing various emotional states. This only served to fuel name calling and threats, and I switched to Sleeping Bears and added an image of a happy bear family. The girls' responded with good absorption in the image. I asked them to "stay sleeping" and invited the parents back into the room, asked them if I could relate a little story, and mom said, "Anything that might help." They adjusted their eyes to the low light. The ocean waves played as I told the family the following story.

Pandora's Box Story

"A long time ago, in ancient Greece, there was a young girl named Pandora. She was given a gift by Zeus, the king of the gods. It was very heavy because it was made of gold and covered with jewels. Zeus told Pandora, 'Whatever you do, don't dare open this box.'

"Time passed and eventually Pandora's curiosity got the best of her. She pried open the box with a sharp rock and immediately she heard a loud rushing sound. The sound continued for several minutes, and then things started flying out of the box, all the evils of the world—hunger, sadness, illness, meanness, and war—and pretty soon the rushing sound stopped and there was silence. Pandora peered into the box. Something bright was shining down there in the bottom of the box. Do you know what it was?"

"It was gold," said Isabella. "No, it was jewelry," countered Elise. "It was *hope*, that's what she saw. *Hope*." "Oh," said mom. "I saw the Hope on TV," said Elise. "That was the *Pope*, stupid," said her sister. "Nice story," said dad.

Follow-up

I called them in three months. "They still pick at each other, but it's nowhere near what it once was," said mom. "Give me a number, zero to 10," I said. "It's never got higher than a two," said mom, who added, "I still want to know *why* they did this." I said, "With many problems we may wonder why, and there's probably no good answer. You did something about the *what*, that's what counts." Six months later it was still "about a two," and I asked them to keep playing the tape at bedtime. I never heard from them again.

THE CASE OF RUSTY

Rusty, age 15, an only child, came in with his parents who complained of his defiance and poor grades in high school. Dad, a former Marine, was a heavy drinker who was unemployed. Rusty's mom worked in the public library.

Rusty was casually dressed and wore a baseball cap backwards on his head. The boy showed vocal and respiratory tics, cardinal features of Tourette's syndrome. His parents indicated that these tics had been present for about one year. Mom worked part-time and had no health insurance. I asked them how they got along and dad said, "Just see if you can get this kid to show some respect." She said they had taken Rusty to a free clinic on the south side of town, and the nurse practitioner had prescribed SSRIs and tranquilizers. "We're not sure if he takes them or not," said mom. "He needs to just grow up," said dad. I told them they needed to take their son to a neurologist. "We'll try," said mom.

Here was a moderately low functioning family who had clearly identified their son as the only problem. Rusty cried as he talked about how kids at school teased him constantly about his grunting and other odd behavior. "My parents just tell me to grow up," he said. His parents had not spoken to personnel at the school about Rusty's problem. "My dad's drunk all the time," he noted.

"What do you do for fun?" I asked. "I *love* hot air balloons. My uncle took me to New Mexico once to watch them. That's what I want to be, a captain of one of those ships," he said. This was the first time I had seen him smile.

Second Session

I saw the parents alone the next session. "I may be able to help Rusty, but dad, you need to do something first: you have to get a hold of your drinking problem. Here's the number you call for help." "I don't have a drinking problem!" he roared before storming out. Mom broke down in tears, and then quietly exited.

A Month Later

On the computerized record system I was alerted to cosign a note from a substance abuse counselor. Dad was getting treatment and had been sober for seven days. I called them and set up an appointment.

At the next session I complimented dad on taking a big step "for the sake of you and your family," explained hypnotic ego strengthening, and asked if I might apply this procedure to Rusty. "Knock yourself out," said dad, as mom looked away.

I explained hypnosis to Rusty and he was eager to begin. As he settled into the recliner he grunted a few times, but then only grunted twice more during the following induction.

Pleasant Image Induction

"Rusty, just let those eyes close as you drift off into a nice, peaceful and comfortable state of *relaxation* . . . I'd like you to imagine a feeling of profound *comfort* up there are the top of your head . . . is that a feeling of warmth or coolness or something else that is oh-so pleasant? When it's there, let me know by nodding your head one time."

He nodded and then I led him through an imaginal muscle relaxation, gradually guiding the pleasant feeling down to the tips of his toes. Then I asked him a question:

"Rusty, beginning now I'd like the back part of your mind to come up with a relaxing image, where you can see yourself, in your mind, feeling *really good*, and I don't know if that's on the beach, or someplace else. . . ."

He nodded his head when he visualized the image and I asked him to tell me what he saw, and sure enough, there he was all alone up there in a hot air balloon.

"We know that a balloon goes where it wants to, but the gas burner, *that* you can control, and that burner, turn it on *now* and let it burn, strong and steady, filling up that balloon, as it travels on its journey. . . ."

Balloons Story III Deepening

Rusty, as you continue on your journey, I want to read you a little story about another kind of balloon, and as you listen to it, you can let your experience of relaxation develop and deepen.

It was a warm spring evening at the State Fair and Frankie's job at the fair was to sell balloons to make money for a special project for the 10th grade at Central High School. Frankie had a large fistful of strings, and attached to each string was a balloon. On each balloon was written a word. On a red balloon was "Happiness." On a green one was "Disapppoint-ment." Other balloons of various colors contained words like "Anger," "Joy," "Doubt," "Hard work," "Fun," and "Fear."

Frankie had walked around the fair for three long hours, and so far he had sold only one balloon. Did that balloon have "Happiness" on it? He couldn't remember. He was getting so tired, and his hand hurt from holding onto all those balloons. It felt like the balloons were fastened to his fist with Superglue. Frankie heard in his head the voice of a trusted friend. "*You can let those balloons go,*" said the voice. He opened his hand just a little and one balloon flew up in to the air. Then his hand opened all by itself and all the remaining balloons, he *just let them go.*

Before realerting I told Rusty: "With that right hand, let that first finger and thumb touch, forming a little circle. This is your anchor . . . when you need to slow down, be strong, take stock of things. . . ." As he was leaving I said, "You're dad's making an effort. Why don't you meet him halfway? Tell him please and thank you for starters, okay?" "Yeah," he said.

Systemic Changes

I saw Rusty three more times. He was using his anchor at school and kids were picking on him less. He assured me he was taking the antidepressant medication, and that it hclped. I employed the "Greenhouse" and other ego strengthening stories (Gafner & Benson, 2003). His mood brightened and he showed more confidence. Dad continued treatment, and mom attended Al-Anon meetings. I called the school counselor about helping him with the grunting, and she was very receptive. She spoke with his teachers, who sent him on regular "errands" during which he released many pent-up grunts. He never did see a neurologist, but that didn't seem to matter.

STORIES FOR CHILDREN

An excellent resource for working with children is Mills and Crowley (1986), *Therapeutic Metaphors for Children and the Child Within.* The authors present a strong rationale for fostering behavior change through unconscious communication by means of metaphor, story, and drawing. I relied on this work when I composed the following induction, which I employ early in therapy with children ages 5 and older. Following the induction is a very versatile story for children, "Tony's Balloons," placed here as a deepening.

The Little Monster Induction

Beginning now, I would like you to close your eyes and let your mind *sleep*, yes, *sleep*, very deeply, as I tell you about the journey of the little monster.

Now, we know that monsters are supposed to be green, green like Shrek. But this little monster was pink, and knowing that he was so *different* from all the other monsters, he felt sad, awkward, left out, and very, very *different*. One night he went to bed and slept very deeply. In his sleep he had a dream.

In the dream he felt very light, his mind and his body both, and he rose up into the sky and drifted off, flying above the clouds. Up there, he floated for what seemed like a *long, long time*. He flew down from the sky and landed in the middle of a family of elephants. "How come you're dragging your leg?" one of the elephants asked him. "Oh, I guess my leg *fell asleep*," answered the little green monster. "How come you're pink?" asked another. "I don't know," answered the little monster. "I was born that way. I've always been pink." Grandfather elephant told him, "If we had a pink elephant he would be *very special*, very special indeed."

The little monster began to rise up again in the sky. "Wait, Pinkie, don't leave so soon," said grandfather elephant. But in no time the little monster was soaring again up into the clouds. "Pinkie, that's *a nice name*," he said to himself. "I like the name Pinkie better than little green monster."

Pinkie didn't know how long he was up there, his body was so light, and his leg still felt *tingly*. It sure felt good to be light as a feather, floating up there in the clouds. Soon he went down again, and this time he came down in the middle of a family of coyotes. "What's your name?" asked mama coyote? "Pinkie," answered the lttle green monster. His body felt *so heavy*, and he felt very *sleepy*. "We don't have any pink coyotes," said daddy coyote. "You must be *very strong*, and a good hunter, too," said daddy coyote. Pinkie smiled, and very soon his body was light again, and up he rose, high up into the sky.

After a *long, long time* Pinkie floated down again, and this time he landed in the middle of some people who were having a picnic. He told them his name, and they said, "Pinkie, you must be hungry, here's a sandwich," and Pinkie bit into the sandwich and swallowed it down. The mother said to him, "Pinkie, being so pink, you must have a lot of *courage*." "'Courage,' what's that?" asked Pinkie. "It means you're *special* and also *very strong*," said the mother, and Pinkie smiled, a big, big smile. Pinkie suddenly rose again, up into the sky, and he continued to float up there for what seemed like hours.

The little monster woke up from his dream in the morning, and he knew that he'd had a dream, but he couldn't remember what was in the dream. At breakfast his mother asked him, "Why do you have a big smile on your face?"

Tony's Balloons Deepening

(Client's name), let your mind sleep even more deeply as you listen to a story called Tony's Balloons.

Not long ago I went to the county fair. I saw a young child 8 or 9 years old holding what looked like a huge umbrella of colorful balloons by a tangle of strings. There must have been hundreds of those balloons.

I said, "Hi there, what's your name?" The child smiled brightly and replied, "Morning, my name's Tony. I'm in third grade and I'm selling balloons." Tony was wearing some faded, holey jeans, a T-shirt with a school logo on the front, and some Nike sneakers. It was still early in the morning and there weren't many people at the fairgrounds yet. I watched Tony as he wandered around with his huge canopy of colorful balloons

Every once in a while he'd ask someone, "Hi, wanna buy a balloon?" Most people said no, and others said they'd buy one later. I could tell he was getting discouraged. He looked longingly at the other kids enjoying the different rides, eating cotton candy and hot dogs. After a while I saw him by one of the tents. He was carefully pulling out the string of an orange balloon. He held it at arm's length, admiring it for the longest time, watching how the breeze played with it, and then he *let it go.*

It rose slowly at first, like it didn't want to leave, but then the wind caught it and it lifted off, up into the sky. At first, it looked like Tony was sad to see the balloon go, but after a moment a smile came on his face, and just then he separated another balloon. This one was rainbow colored. He let it go quickly and watched as it was carried away out of sight. This was fun!

Next, he pulled out five more balloons, a blue one, a pink one, and other colors. He *just let them go.* They floated up and seemed to play tag with each other, and then drifted away. Some grown-ups and children noticed what he was doing and they gathered close for a better look.

All of a sudden an idea came to Tony. He opened up his hand and he released all the rest of the balloons. He laughed with glee. He had let them go, every last one (Jacobs, personal communication, 2006).

Clinical Comments

There may be more opportunities to apply hypnosis to the problems of children and adolescents than to adults. When we think of hypnosis with adults we usually imagine a quiet setting with the lights turned low, the therapist speaking softly to the client, who sits passively in a recliner with eyes closed and feet up.

Certainly the adult scenario may apply to children ages 10 and older; however, the majority of your hypnotic work with children will be far from something calm, controlled, and passive. Olness and Cohen (1996) compiled a list of induction techniques for children and adolescents ages 2 to 18, and these techniques include tactile stimulation such as stroking and patting, blowing bubbles, storytelling, television fantasy, playground activity, and eye fixation. In one major way hypnosis with children is like hypnosis with adults: The route to intervention is attentional absorption, or induction; however, the routes for children are more manifold.

5

Directive Inductions

Although this book emphasizes indirection, embedded suggestion, and metaphor, let's keep in mind that many practitioners in the United States and abroad employ only highly directive inductions. Since the 1800s, hypnotic induction has meant eliciting hypnotic phenomena by such means as eye roll (e.g., "Follow my hand with your eyes as I move it up over your forehead. As your eyes roll up they *will* close and you *will* drop into a very deep trance"). Authoritarian words like *will* are operative, as opposed to *can* or *may* in permissive inductions. With the promulgation of Milton Erickson's work since the 1970s, indirect suggestions and permissive language have become popular in many circles.

Is one method better? No—and yes! There is some evidence that clients who are less hypnotizable may respond better to indirection. Also, the clinical experience of many therapists indicates that clients who are reactant may respond better to indirection. Clearly, directive inductions like arm catalepsy or hand levitation (Gafner & Benson, 2000) are very quick compared to long, conversational-type inductions, and the ability of directive inductions to produce hypnotic phenomena can be a rapid convincer of trance.

Clients may have physical problems that contraindicate the use of directive inductions. People with joint pain may not like progressive muscle relaxation, where muscle groups are tensed and relaxed, just as people with lung or airway disease may begin to cough if your induction emphasizes deep breathing. Clients with diseases of the eye or arthritis in the neck may not like the eye roll induction, just as people with cervical pain or peripheral neuropathy may dislike the Coin Drop or Arm Catalepsy inductions.

In my experience with thousands of clients of all ages I believe that *most* people, if given the choice, will appreciate indirect inductions over directive ones because they are gentle, permissive, and respectful of individual differences. They allow people to experience trance as they wish. For sure, *some* people will want, or expect, a directive induction. In our training program interns learn to apply both types, and because they are important I have included four directive inductions in this book.

These guided imagery inductions are a bridge between traditional, authoritarian inductions, such as eye roll or arm catalepsy, and their polar opposite, permissive and indirect routes to trance, such as story inductions. They are directive in that a guided framework for experience is provided, but absorption occurs in the imagery and less so in the physicality of the hypnotic phenomena. Flowing to the Sea, is adapted from a handout by Rob Narke at a 1997 American Society of Clinical Hypnosis conference in California. The Pyramid is attributed to Gibbons (1979) and was elucidated by Stanton (1985). The third induction, The Forest, encourages absorption in the natural world. These three inductions are directive in that the details are provided by the therapist, as opposed to an indirect induction where the client's imagination fills in the blanks. The language in these inductions encourages clients to overcome obstacles and to retrieve internal resources, such as past learnings. Some people may appreciate the structure provided by guided imagery, while others may experience it as heavy-handed or trite. If a client responds well to one of these, I usually repeat it in subsequent sessions.

Contrast the direct presentation of images and relative absence of hypnotic language in these inductions with story inductions, which are driven by embedded suggestion, devices such as apposition of opposites, story within a story, and emphasis of *another's* experience as metaphor. Here, the metaphor is linear, frank, and unadorned, and all suggestions are directed at *you*, the subject.

FLOWING TO THE SEA

Whenever you employ an induction with high specificity you run the risk of something striking the client as incongruent or negative. For example, once I used this induction with a client after taking a poor history. He spontaneously realerted midway and declined to continue. As a youth he had experienced a terrifying near-drowning. "Okay then, I'll use some material where water isn't even mentioned," I said. "No, thanks, you've helped me quite enough," he responded.

We live and learn. Most clients, however, become pleasantly absorbed in this guided imagery exercise and discover long forgotten resources, or something else stimulated by the sea metaphor.

Flowing to the Sea Induction

I would like you to start out by taking two deep, refreshing breaths, and with the second exhalation you can let those eyes close, as you begin to drift off into a nice, *pleasant, comfortable* trance.

As you relax in the silence, you find yourself in a forest, any forest at all. It is quiet and peaceful and at your feet you discover a bubbling spring. You are gazing into this fresh, cool spring water. Warm sunshine filters through the tall trees, green moss is growing on the rocks, and the birds sing softly in the branches above. You feel especially calm and peaceful in this place, and you are one with nature. Amidst this calmness there is something else. There is a special *excitement* in the air, the excitement of new beginnings.

The bubbling spring seems to be singing, singing a clear melody in a vibrant rhythm. It is the rhythm of life, adventure, and discovery. You notice a small current flowing from the spring, and you feel drawn to this moving current. You bend down to hear its secret song. You dangle your hand in the coolness and you notice a tiny twig in the swirling waters of the stream. The twig is spinning around and around, and as you watch it, you also spin down *deeper* and *deeper* into a soothing *sleep*. Deeper and deeper into a most pleasing sleep.

The twig is caught in the backwash circles of life, spinning around in an endless turn of events. You wonder what life would be like downstream, what new insights lie downstream. Could new joys, knowledge, experiences, and adventure await you downstream? Suddenly your hand lifts the tiny twig out of the whirlpool and that hand drops it into the middle of the stream, into the mainstream of life. You feel a sudden rush of energy flow through your body. You are free! You are the tiny twig, flowing downstream, moving along at a lively pace, bobbing and weaving along with the bubbling current in search of the open sea.

The trickling stream now grows wider and wider, and you are merging with other streams, as you flow down into the valley. You are no longer just a tiny twig, for you are now the stream, surging downward and forward, following the path that nature has opened in your path. Your waters are merging with other streams of energy, growing stronger and stronger, moving along into wider channels of *confidence*, and you feel an overwhelming sense of *satisfaction*.

Your inner force is growing wider and deeper, and the banks are reaching out. Your *sleep deepens* as you become a mighty river of natural clearness, moving eagerly onward, rushing forward with great satisfaction. Anticipation builds along with new *energy, freedom,* and *growth.* You experience a new life of creative transformation, adventure, and new beginnings. You continue to merge with other rivers, flowing easily and surely, *freer and freer*, and your deep sleep continues, dreaming and drifting.

In no time at all you arrive at the sea, a sea of boundless abundance. You feel peaceful and content as you become one with the sea. What is the name of this sea? It is the Sea of Forever, and you hear quite clearly its majestic music of serenity, its melody of freedom, fulfillment, and joy.

Images Deepening

Images of river and sea, and feelings of confidence, freedom, and growth, these are things in which you can further immerse yourself, becoming further absorbed, deeper and deeper. Just let your experience continue to *deepen* now, and I will resume speaking again in a little while.

THE PYRAMID

Most guided-imagery inductions are linear, clearly stated, and very goal-directed. They are very different from story inductions, which may have meandering stories within stories and contain embedded suggestions, misspeak, and other devices. Story inductions usually encourage the listener to become absorbed in someone else's experience, whereas directive inductions like the Pyramid are about the client. Clients who appreciate an adventure or journey in which they are the protagonist may get immersed in the following induction.

The Pyramid Induction

You may sit back and close your eyes if you wish, for in a moment I'm going to ask you to generate an image in your mind. That's the way.... Beginning now, I would like you to picture yourself, in your mind, in ancient Egypt, standing before a gigantic pyramid, gazing at an opening in the side. It is nighttime and a sand storm is whirling about you. You feel the sand stinging your cheeks and you quickly step inside. It is *quiet* and *cool* inside, but in no time you feel your feet moving and you are propelled forward.

You enter a well-lit passageway that leads downward. You feel safe and secure in here. As you move forward, the wind outside becomes barely audible, and soon you cannot hear it at all. You continue walking, ever downward, and suddenly you feel a sense of *excitement* and *expectancy*. Something of immense value is about to be experienced.

You drift and dream as you continue pacing ever downward. Everyday awareness is left far behind. You trudge onward, your legs moving all by themselves. A long time seems to have passed, but in reality only a few minutes have elapsed. You come to the end of the passageway and there you encounter a vast storehouse of treasures, piles of gold and silver coins, and manifold chests overflowing with jewels. But wait! Something very bright impedes you and you must shield your eyes. A pulsing luminescence throbs from the midst of the treasure trove. You see a massive silver statue on guard. This guardian is powered by a brilliant jewel in its forehead and its light blocks your way.

The treasures are yours for the taking were it not for the sentinel and its powerful light. Suddenly you are overtaken by fatigue and you sit down, bathed in the amber light from the guardian. Your body extends itself on the floor and in no time you are fast asleep. You sleep very deeply. In your dream you encounter a way to bypass the guardian. You awake with a start and then your work begins, as you gather up a measureless quantity of treasure. You walk back up the passageway and emerge outside. It is daytime now and the sun is shining. You walk away with renewed confidence, and you also have something else: a *wonderful joy of discovery.*

Helgason Deepening

I would like you to let your experience deepen as I tell you a little story about a ground squirrel. One day a young boy was in a daydream, ambling absentmindedly through a field near his home. His reverie was broken by something that caught his attention off to the right: It was a ground squirrel that had popped out of his hole. He stopped and stared at the little squirrel for the longest time. He wondered about all the things beneath the ground, things known only to the little squirrel, who communicated many things without words (Helgason, 2006).

THE FOREST

I use this induction with clients who are "therapy junkies," travelers who never arrive—they are in your office, you're their 25th therapist, and you're supposed to fix them. However, I also use it with people who are searching for answers, and many times the structure of this induction allows people to discover something meaningful. The onus is on the client, where it should be. In many ways this induction is like an ambiguous function assignment, a strategic therapy technique that is eminently useful with people who are searching for something.

The Forest Induction

You can sit back and close those eyes, if you wish, as we begin this guided experience, and I would like you to imagine, *just imagine*, a feeling of profound and soothing comfort beginning down at the soles of your feet. I don't know if that image of comfort is warm or cool, liquid or solid, abstract or literal, but it can be anything at all, and whatever it is, just let it happen now, going up your body, slowly or rapidly, up one leg first, or up both legs at the same time, and I will be quiet for a few moments while this relaxation occurs, effortlessly, independently, automatically, and unconsciously.

It is a warm, sunny day, and you find yourself now in a beautiful forest, you've been here before, and you know it is a safe place. You feel absolutely *wonderful* as you start down a path on this *journey of discovery*. You walk for a couple of minutes, stop, and reach into your right pocket. You open the folded piece of paper which says, "Count down now, in your mind, from 20 to 10, 20 . . . 19 . . . , that's the way, sinking *deeper and deeper* into a most delightful sense of relaxation. . . ." You place the paper into your left pocket and continue down the path, anticipating the joy of discovery that you know lies ahead.

Your pace is brisk on the path as you penetrate *deeper and deeper* into the forest, and you marvel at your newfound depth of relaxtion, comfort, and well-being. You feel the life of the forest, the scents and sounds, and marvel at this most remarkable experience. You stop and reach into your right pocket for the second slip of paper, which says, "Continue counting down, in your mind, from 10 to 1," and your *experience deepens* even more.

There is a spring in your step and your body feels relaxed and heavy, but this incongruence is reconciled by your expectancy of what lies ahead. Your feet are propelled forward, moving all by themselves. The sunshine is filtered by the leaves, but the position of the sun is unclear. Is it still morning or has afternoon already arrived? Have you been in the woods for mere moments, or have hours passed? Losing track of time is of no consequence, as you glide down the path. Your oneness with the natural world is now reaching a profound depth of curiosity and appreciation.

A crunching beneath your feet alerts you to small stones in the path. You leave your reverie for a moment as you notice a fork in the trail. Do you go right, or should you take the path to the left? You stop, breathe deeply, and reach in your pocket one more time. Unfolding the slip of paper you read the words, and quickly turn down the right path.

You continue on, effortless steps in timeless motion, and you drift and dream. In your dream an *indescribable clarity* penetrates your consciousness. Something old and familiar has suddenly taken on *new meaning*. This discovery provides you with an immeasurable comfort, and you bask in this wonderful light of undersanding and satisfaction. You continue down the path, which is now nearing its end. Familiar faces up ahead are eager to greet you. Words resound in your head, and those words say, "I must take something with me to remember this day!" What comes to mind is a complete *surprise*, a *gift* from today's experience.

African Violets Deepening

You may let your imagination drift, dream, and deepen as I tell you about Dr. Erickson's visit to the home of an elderly woman in Milwaukee, Wisconsin. He used a cane and walked with a limp as he toured the home, noticing that the curtains were drawn and the house was dark except for one window, in which grew a tray of beautiful African Violets. Erickson made a mental note of these flowers.

Dr. Erickson never saw the woman again, but he said one thing to her before he left, which was, "Grow some of those beautiful flowers for your friends." We can only imagine how much light came into the house as she grew more and more of the flowers. In fact, she became known as the African Violet Queen of Milwaukee.

REMORSE, LOSS, AND FORGIVENESS

Clients often seek help from a therapist after they have attempted other measures to solve their problem. For people who are unable to let go of guilt, or to forgive themselves, I usually first employ ego strengthening measures, often followed by the "Balloons" story (Gafner, 2004; Gafner & Benson, 2000), which embeds letting go. Next, I might lead clients through an age regression exercise to help them see how they felt *before* the advent of the problem, or age progression, so they might see themselves in the future with the problem resolved. I might also set up finger signals and ask a series of questions of the unconscious mind (e.g., "Is there some reason you can't let go of this problem?").

For people who have a need to punish themselves for a wrong they have committed, I may ask them to see a movie, *The Mission*. In the movie, a man has killed his brother and he asks a priest how he can forgive himself for this terrible sin. The priest assigns a physical ordeal. As he goes about completing the task, he asks the priest how he will know when he has suffered enough, and he is told that *only he will know* when he has paid sufficient penance.

Many client problems seem to belong to an existential or spiritual realm. Resolution may lie in the following induction, Remorse, which may more aptly be called a meditation. Repeated practice may lead to a diminution of the problem, which some may interpret as desensitization, while others may view as problem solving on a spiritual or unconscious level. Whatever it is, the therapist places responsibility for resolution on the client, which is where it belongs. I give the following induction to clients on a tape, but I also give it to them on paper, as a set of instructions for practice. Many clients require some office sessions practicing it before doing it at home.

Remorse Induction

Find a familiar, quiet, comfortable place, either outside or inside.

Begin by taking some cleansing, refreshing breaths. Gently close your eyes and allow complete relaxation to fill your body and your mind. Use any helpful images or memories to assist you.

Count silently from 20 to 1, very slowly, appreciating how your experience deepens with each number descending down.

Imagine a light, perhaps a white light or some other color, shining down on you from above. Your body and your mind are bathed in this healing light. With each breath in you feel more and more of its radiance.

Picture yourself sitting across from you. Yes, you are looking at yourself from several feet away. Focus on the problem (guilt, need for self-forgiveness, need to let go, etc.). This problem is very strong. It has been with you for a long time and may have served some purpose, but you no longer need it, at least not *all* of it. You only require a small portion of it as a reminder of your suffering. You can let it go, yes, *just let it go*. Take a few moments and concentrate on this letting go.

Now, return your attention to the light and see yourself the way you want to be from now on. Feel that healing light on your mind, on your body, and especially on your heart. Say to yourself, "Yes, I can move on with my life."

Breathe in very deeply and exhale.

You feel that healing light, you feel it especially on your hands. Are those hands hot or merely warm? Let that heat develop in your hands. Place your hands over your heart and say, "Yes, I *can* move on with my life."

Relax those hands, allow them to sit on your lap. Breathe in deeply and exhale, and let your mind sleep, as long as you want, and when you have slept sufficiently, your eyes will open. You are alert, refreshed, and reinvigorated (Stratton, 1997).

Clinical Comments

I use no deepening with Remorse, as people tend to deepen their experience with continued practice. Contrast the simplicity and directness of Remorse with hours and hours of talking about letting go in conventional psychotherapy. Of course, a symptom like guilt may also be amenable to strategic techniques such as ordeal, ambiguous function assignment, Greek Chorus, or similar techniques (Gafner & Benson, 2002).

If you like directive inductions, I encourage you to try Arm Catalepsy, Coin Drop, and similar inductions in *The Handbook of Hypnotic Inductions*

(Gafner & Benson, 2000). If you do needlework, carpentry, or automotive repair, you appreciate the *right tool* for the job. In some cases, a directive induction is that right tool, and it's good to have it handy for when you might need it.

6

Confusional Inductions

In the range of hypnotic induction, at one extreme we have clients who *do not want* to go into trance. That's easy: We don't do hypnosis with these clients. Next on the continuum we have clients who go into trance easily with minimal effort expended by the therapist: "Beginning now, let yourself become absorbed in your favorite image, and when you are sufficiently deep, let me know by nodding your head." This is the essence of the law of parsimony: more is less, and do only what is necessary to achieve the desired response. Then, we have clients perhaps new to trancework, and most of them respond to either story or directive inductions.

On the other end of the continuum we have clients who do not respond to story or other inductions. They *want* to go into trance, but can't do so because they are resistant at an *unconscious* level. These clients are among the approximately 10% of the U.S. population who are deemed nonhypno-tizable. As noted earlier, I estimate that we can cut that rate to 5% by employing confusional inductions. If people do not respond to them, I recommend an approach other than hypnosis.

FOUR FACES

I use confusional inductions rarely, maybe 2–3% of the time, and generally only when they are indicated. However, I occasionally use Four Faces with a long-term client, say, a person with chronic depression whom I see supportively for ego-strengthening, stress management, or exploration. This induction can tend to perturb, a good thing with most clients, and it is also good—both for therapists and clients—to occasionally try something novel or different, something outside the comfort zone.

Four Faces Induction

We use this induction to test clients' ability to just let go and experience trance in whatever way they'd like. Accordingly, you may sit back, close your eyes, and appreciate the following account in your own way.

It was the winter of 1983 at the plenary demonstration of the Lankton Consortium in The Hague, Switzerland. The renowned scholar, Dr. Detour Delaney, was on stage with four subjects whom he would put into trance in front of the large audience of doctors. Cameras projected Dr. Delaney and the faces of the subjects onto an oversized screen at the rear of the stage.

Delaney was introduced to a burst of applause. He was a capacious man in suspenders and his commanding voice could have been heard even without a microphone.

"You may dim the lights now," he directed. The *four faces* on the screen were prominent and the exit lights glowed off to the side.

Delaney stepped forward and took the arm of the first subject, a woman with icy blue eyes. "Madam, I shall *take your arm* like this," he said with a flair, as he extended her right arm out in front of her. "You may close your eyes now and begin to turn your attention inward, to your body, that's the way. . . ." The hand on your lap, the arm in the air, I *wonder* what sensations that hand on your lap *can develop* while that arm is in the air, *how long* will it take to descend to the comfort of your lap?

The extended arm made little sinking movements and the doctor continued: "I want you to *NOT allow* that arm to descend all the way to your lap *UNTIL you're ready* to drift off into the most peaceful of trances . . . *a woman* I was working with just yesterday in my office, she *detected* the most curious sensations in her feet. . . ."

Icy Blue Eyes took one deep, refreshing breath and then her arm descended, down, all the way. Many in the audience had now closed their eyes, while the other three subjects on stage observed with marked inquisitiveness. "*Sleep very deeply now*," he said to the first subject.

Delaney turned to the audience and said, "You may observe goings-on *up here* while at the same time you experience trance in your own way *down there*. People *up here* often experience at least a moderate depth of trance,

metaphor

arm catalepsy

power word

implication

direct question

contingent suggestion

metaphor

suggestion

suggestion

apposition of opposites

while you, *out there*, can go deep inside, notic-
ing *specific sensations* in your own body, or   *suggestion*
mind, a qualitative depth of experience both
individually and collectively. The faces on the
screen now glowed in a purple hue and Native
American flute music began to pulsate softly
from the back of the auditorium, or was it
from the side? Delaney had forgotten about
the music. "*A very nice touch*," he thought to   *fluff*
himself. He was silent for several moments
while he collected his thoughts.

Delaney shifted his attention to the next
subject, a man with bushy eyebrows. Without
speaking to him he glanced down at the man's
left hand, moving his head *slightly up* and   *suggestion*
down as if somehow coaxing the man's hand
upward, and soon discernible lifting move-
ments occurred, and the *hand began to move*   *hand levitation*
up. "Sir, the lights have dimmed, but we are
interested in another kind of *light*, the remark-
able *lightness* developing rapidly now in that   *suggestion*
left hand. Yes, just like that, let that hand con-
tinue on its journey upward, and *when* it has   *contingent suggestion*
reached its desired height, your *eyes may close*
and you can *drift off* into the most wonderful
of trances."

The audience was now completely still and
the flute music played on. Delaney stepped
past the third subject and addressed the
fourth. "They don't call me Detour for nothing," he whispered, glancing back at Icy Blue
Eyes, arm in the air, chin on her chest, and
Bushy Eyebrows, hand levitated and in a state
of deep reverie.

The fourth subject was a young woman

with a pageboy haircut. Delaney had begun
the program speaking in a rather loud, expan-
sive voice, and now he spoke in a mere whisper. Pageboy appeared nervous as her eyes
darted about the room. Delaney continued,
"Miss, being up here on stage has set the stage
for the deepest of trances. It may seem like
those eyes out there are *boring* into you, but   *pun*
most of those eyes have already closed, and the
few that remain open can become *boring*, as
indeed, such *boredom* heralds the most pleas-
ant of *reveries*. Pageboy's eyes closed, Delaney   *suggestion*
whispered something in her ear, and in no time
her chin was on her chest.

He stepped back to subject number three, a
young man in T-shirt and shorts, whose eyes
were closed. "Sir," he said, "*perhaps* you've   *implication*
already become *absorbed* in a pleasant image,
and I don't know if in that image you are *walk-*   *suggestion covering all*
ing along the beach, *watching* a movie, or   *possibilities*
some other enjoyable activity. *Isn't* total men-
tal immersion the most wonderful of things?"   *direct question*

Delaney stepped away from the four faces,
all now deep in trance. He gazed out at the
audience, which was *quiet and unmoving*. "A   *catalepsy*
timeless void, most pleasant indeed," he said.

Our account of the proceedings does not
provide what Delaney did next. Years later a
Delaney associate *wrote in her memoirs* that in   *fluff*
the master's demonstrations he usually sig-
naled for the *music to stop*, and that often he
began a long, boring story, and other times *re-*
alerted subjects by counting from one up to   *distraction*
five. She also noted that Delaney customarily
said some familiar words at the conclusion:

"Before you come back to the present *I would like you to consult* your unconscious mind, asking this deepest part of you for *a gift*, yes, a gift, to remember today's experience, something to assist you in the future. But you don't have to know now what that gift is. You need only *say "yes"* inwardly to yourself and your unconscious mind will do the rest, letting this suggestion percolate in a most mysterious and intriguing way. This gift *may soon surface* to your conscious mind, or perhaps it will be two weeks from now. Will it be a *word, a sound, an idea*, or *something else?*"

    suggestion

    suggestion

    suggestion covering all possibilities

    And for you, now and here, (client's name), I would like you to conclude your experience today by taking *two refreshing breaths*, after which you may resume your alert, waking state when you are ready to do so. *But wait!* Please don't take those two deep breaths just yet, as I have a few more words to say to you, and you may *let your experience deepen* as you listen to those words now.

    suggestion

    distraction

    suggestion

Direct Question Deepening

The famous Dr. Erickson was fond of saying to people, "Your conscious mind is smart, but your *unconscious* mind is much wiser." I know that we're not at the beginning, but he often asked people at the start, "Regarding your experience today, are you ready to go into a mild trance, a medium trance, or a deep trance?"

LEFT RIGHT

This induction takes off from other similar inductions over the years. An earlier version of this can be found in *Handbook of Hypnotic Inductions*.

I sometimes employ another therapist in this induction, with each of us alternating reading it. I did this once with a client and he didn't go into trance. The next time we told him we would repeat the induction. We read it again, alternating arts, stopped briefly at the end, and then just *one person* launched into a second reading of it. The client drifted off into trance this time. Thereafter all that was needed for successful hypnosis was one therapist and story inductions. Such is often the case: after you break through the resistance, a confusional induction is no longer needed.

Left Right Induction

I would like you to listen to the following account, and as you do so, you may close your eyes, if you wish. We usually recommend that people *not listen* to the words, and if you don't,	*restraint*
you may choose instead to pay attention to *any feelings* that develop in your body.	*suggestion*
Two men named Wright and Leftkovitz, also known as Lefty, had long sought the *perfect state*. After seeking and not finding this	*pun*
place for many years, they sought counsel from a wise, elderly *woman*, who guaranteed	*metaphor*
them that they would find the perfect state if they followed some precise directions. These directions were, "Take two rights and two lefts. Simply that, two rights and two lefts. But you *may not be ready* for this, *am I right?*	*restraint; direct question*
They set out in Wright's automobile with Lefty driving, and they took a *right*, a *left*, a *right* and a *left*, but they did not find it. They next took two *lefts* and two *rights* and Lefty	*confusion*
said to Wright, "Are we any closer?" Wright answered, "Maybe a little closer, but we must keep on." It was a *warm sunny* day with not much traffic and Wright said, "Lefty, just be	*fluff*

patient." After one *left*, Wright said, "Let me drive," and they then completed a *right* turn followed by a *left*, another *left*, and one more *right*, and still they did not find what they were looking for. *confusion*

Then they decided to try something different. Lefty sat in the *right* front, then the *left* rear, and they resumed driving. They completed two *lefts* and two *rights*, then two *rights* and two *lefts*, but still did not get there. *confusion*

Lefty said, "Wright, when I drive, try sitting behind me for one *right*, opposite me for one *left*, and then in the *right* passenger seat, until I complete the required turns." "Okay, maybe that will work," responded Wright, but still they were *left* without finding the *right* place. *confusion* Wright placed himself behind the wheel again, with Lefty in the front passenger seat, and they took a *right*, a *left*, a *right* and another *left*, but that didn't work either. Wright remained behind the wheel with Lefty sitting where he wanted, and they took a *right*, a *left*, a *left*, and *confusion* another *right*, still without success.

"We *have* to be getting closer," muttered Lefty, but Wright did not hear him. As Wright accelerated into a *left* turn, he took a *right*, a *left*, a *left* and a *right*, followed by a *left*, a *right*, a *right* and a *left*, but still they did get there. Lefty slid over to the rear passenger seat as Wright bent to his task, *perplexed* by an *suggestion* increasingly *exasperating* situation. He took a *right*, a *left*, a *right* and a *left*, and then reversed the order, a *left*, *right*, a *left*, and a *right*, then three *rights* and one *left*, followed by three *lefts* *confusion* and one *right*. "You're not following the directions," said Lefty, and just then Wright braked hard, pulled off the road, sat back, and closed his eyes.

In the back seat, Lefty did the same, and soon they *drifted off* into another state.   *suggestion*

Direct Question II Deepening

You can let your experience deepen as I ask you a couple of questions. First, when Napoleon invaded Russia, he probably noticed birds migrating overhead, and shouldn't he have known that winter was arriving early? Also, the boxwood tree, did you know that it only grows one leaf at a time?

Clinical Comments

I always tell clients that I will be using an induction "that might not make sense . . . and that this approach is undertaken to help you go into trance. . . to get in beneath the radar." It is framed as helping, and the rationale is explained. People accept this just fine. After all, they're here for help and they trust you, and just remember, as Peggy Papp (1983) sagely said: "Good doctors do not prescribe bad medicine."

I sometimes use a confusional realerting, which reinforces the overall distraction of a confusional induction. For example, "In a moment, I'm going to count from one up to five at which time you can resume your alert, waking state. 1, 2, 3, 4 and 5." Or, I say I'm going to count from one to five and I say, "4 and 5." Or, I tell them I'm going to count, but I *don't* count at all, but simply say, "Okay, open your eyes now!" This arrests attention—and distracts—as does employing a quick realerting and immediately launching into something irrelevant, such as, "This rug in here, do you think it needs to be vacuumed?"

Many times we strive to be purposeful in inductions, thinking that *all our words* should be directed at the target. However, our suggestions may be more effective if we include some fluff, or meaningless material as filler. Also, let's remember that people are socialized to pay attention, and respond to a direct question. Employing a direct question in an induction creates a temporary confusion, as people search for an answer.

What about using a confusional induction early on? Definitely not, it's not indicated. Try the straightforward ones first. Remember, *most* people will respond to the other inductions.

SEEING THE COLORS

Notice that restraint is offered right at the beginning of this induction. A restraining message is often added with a client who is ambivalent or unconsciously resistant. Early on in conventional talk therapy a client may be reluctant to delve into highly personal matters, so here, too, it may be helpful to tell the client something like, "In the first session many wish to hold back at least 25%, and that's OK."

A Confusional Induction

Beginning now, I'd like you to sit back, close those eyes, and let yourself drift off, not into a moderate or deep trance, but into only a *very light trance* because I will need you to pay close attention to what I'm about to tell you about colors, yes, colors.

Sometimes we don't see what we're looking at, and although this may not apply to you, I'd like you to listen as I tell you about an experiment done some years back at the Lankton Institute. There, they had the subject, Opal Azure, hold in front of her a page-sized chart on which were written the words *red, green, blue,* and *yellow.* However, these words were not painted in the same color as the color the word represented, that is, the word *blue* was colored yellow, yellow was blue, green was red, and red was green.

Dr. Lankton asked the subject to quickly say each word, and Opal did so, going through the words one at a time, rapidly the first time, and even faster the second time. "Yellow-blue-red-green," she said. It was evident to Dr. Lankton right away that errors were occurring. Opal just couldn't get it right. Her experience, was, in fact, similar to hundreds of other subjects; for example, they would read green, but say red, no matter how hard they tried to concentrate.

Now, (client's name), perhaps you have already noticed how your rate of breathing has begun to change, and although your mind is active and alert, something *interesting* has begun to occur in your body, and I don't know if that's a curious sensation in one hand or the other. Maybe your feet feel especially *heavy*, or perhaps your body has *sunk deeper* into that chair. And it really doesn't matter what feelings are there in your body, as they can be observed, by your mind, as if watching something develop at a distance, though we know for certain that there is very little distance between your mind and your body. *Sleep*, profound and restful sleep, how near is it?

Remember now, blue is yellow, yellow is blue, green is red, and reading red, in your mind, it is colored green. I'm not asking you to fix this in your memory just yet, but for now, just picture in your mind, the words, but not in any particular color, the words *yellow-blue-green-red,* or even in reverse order, *red-green-blue-yellow,* and you may nod your head one time when those words are there, in your mind . . . (pause). That's the way. . . .

At the Lankton Institute, Opal attempted the experiment several more times, and eventually asked if she could take a break. She sat by herself in the lounge and *dozed off,* and continued to sleep for what seemed to be the longest time, dreaming dreams only known to her deepest self.

Now, (client's name), I would like you to see again in your mind those words, but painted in the color of the original experiment: blue painted yellow, red in green, yellow in blue, and green in red. Just let it happen there in your mind. . . .

While Opal slept, a discussion ensued among the researchers. A woman argued that trance could be induced through physical movement, such as walking. "Walking meditation is really quite effective," she noted. One man stated that any conveyance on land, or water, or even up in the air, could produce the desired state, while another argued that absorption in a story was the route to trance. Dr. Benson noted, "I am fond of inducing trance by reading from the Saint Paul telephone directory, starting at the back." Dr. Weyer, a senior researcher who was known to induce trance by reading from a textbook on statistics, said, "*Mental* conveyance is the route to trance, which can be like an entrance into another state." Two of the researchers nodded, trying hard to stay awake. They weren't quite sure what he meant by "mental conveyance."

Now, (client's name), take a couple of nice deep breaths, for we know that for many people some refreshing breaths have a distinct deepening effect, and for some the colors may appear more vivid or distinct following two—not one or three—but two, deep, refreshing breaths . . . that's the way . . . and allow yourself to retrieve once more in your mind those familiar colors, green which is really red, yellow/blue, red/green, and blue/yellow.

When Opal awoke she reentered the testing room. She did not realize that she was in for a surprise. Dr. Lankton himself was there, and he asked her to hold a placard on which was added a third color, purple. The word *red* was printed with purple letters on a green background, the word *yellow* was in purple on a blue background, the word *green*, which was purple, appeared on a red background, and *blue* was shown similarly, etched in purple against a background of yellow. Opal's mind swam as she tried in vain to verbalize the correct response.

She was now feeling quite exasperated. She thought about how the traffic light went from yellow to red before the turn arrow came on, or was it the turn arrow that preceded the red light? Opal closed her eyes, sat back, took one deep breath, and just let herself drift off, and *sleep* soon followed.

Balloons Story I Deepening

You can let your experience deepen as I tell you about Deborah, who was a freshman at the University of Michigan in the 1950s. Deborah didn't have a lot of money and one of her part-time jobs was selling concessions at university sporting events, hot chocolate, popcorn, and soft drinks. It was now late October, the day of the homecoming football game, and the boss said to her, "Come with me. I have special duty for you down on the field."

Down there, in the corner of the end zone, she gazed at hundreds of thousands of small balloons of various colors straining beneath a gigantic net. The boss said, "Young woman, your one job today is this: When the players come back on the field to start the second half, you pull hard on this cord right here and *let all those balloons go.*" Deborah nodded, as this was going to be a very easy job.

She had never been much of a football fan, and she ignored the game and the cheers of the crowd. Unaccustomed to cold weather, she vigorously rubbed her hands together, stamped her feet, and through her cold breath she observed the mountain of balloons under the net. Being a curious and imaginative person, Deborah began to wonder what it would be like if *only one balloon* were released ahead of all the others. She toyed with the net, and soon there was enough room for it to escape. As she *let it go*, it quickly rose up in the frigid air and soon the swift currents carried it out of the stadium. She went around to the other side of the net and did the same with a blue balloon, she just *let it go*. She was so absorbed in this activity that she didn't hear the arrival of half time, nor did she hear the roar of the crowed as the players streamed back on the field to start the second half. Suddenly the boss yelled to her, "Pull the cord!" She snapped back to her senses, yanked hard on the cord, and all the remaining balloons, she *just let them go*.

Clinical Comments

A deepening is like fabric softener added to the clothes drier. It's not absolutely essential, but it makes a difference and you come to rely on it. Let's remember that some practitioners employ no formal deepening and their hypnosis sessions have no discernible components, with the induction and therapy being rolled into one. I encourage you to experiment to see what works for you and your clients. With some clients you may wish to lengthen the session—and deepen the client's experience—by attaching a story, say, an ego strengthening story (Gafner, 2004; Gafner & Benson, 2003); however, this may not be necessary. Let your client's response be the guide.

For Further Study

I regularly read the *American Journal of Clinical Hypnosis* (www. asch.net); *Contemporary Hypnosis*, a publication of the British Society of Experimental and Clinical Hypnosis (www.bsech.com); and the *International Journal of Clinical and Experimental Hypnosis* (www.ijech.educ.wsu). Another fine journal is the *Australian Journal of Clinical and Experimental Hypnosis* (www.ozhypnosis.com.au). Additional resources are the British Society of Medical and Dental Hypnosis (www.bsmdh.org) and the Royal Society of Medicine, Section for Hypnosis and Psychosomatic Medicine (www.vsm.ac.uk). Some newsletters, such as those of The International Society of Hypnosis (www.ish.unimelb.edu.au) or the Milton H. Erickson Foundation (www.erickson-foundation.org), can help you keep abreast of developments in the field.

I continue to learn a great deal from many books on hypnosis. Some of these are listed below:

Hypnosis: Questions and Answers, by Bernie Zilbergeld, M. Gerald Edelstien, and Dan Araoz

The Letters of Milton H. Erickson, by Jeff Zeig and Brent Geary

Brief Therapy: Myths, Methods, and Metaphors, by Jeffrey Zeig and Stephen Gilligan, Eds.

Ericksonian Methods: The Essence of the Story, by Jeffrey Zeig, Ed.

Ericksonian Psychotherapy, vols. I and II, by Jeff Zeig, Ed.

Treating Depression with Hypnosis and *Trancework: An Introduction to the Practice of Clinical Hypnosis,* by Michael Yapko

Resolving Sexual Abuse, by Yvonne Dolan

Handbook of Hypnotic Suggestions and Metaphors, by D. C. Hammond

The Psychobiology of Mind-Body Healing, by Ernest Rossi

Mind-Body Therapy, by ErnestRossi and David Cheek

Therapeutic Metaphors for Children and the Child Within, by Joyce Mills and Richard Crowley

Therapeutic Trances and *The Legacy of Milton H. Erickson: Selected Papers of Stephen Gilligan*

In Search of Solutions, by Bill O'Hanlon and Michelle Wiener-Davis

A Brief Guide to Brief Therapy, by Bill O'Hanlon and Brian Cade

Assembling Ericksonian Therapy, by Stephen Lankton

The Answer Within: Clinical Framework of Ericksonian Hypnotherapy, by Stephen Lankton and Carol Lankton

Tales of Enchantment: Goal-Oriented Metaphors for Adults and Children in Therapy, by Stephen Lankton and Carol Lankton

and, last but not least, the valuable works of Milton H. Erickson, two of which are *Hypnotic Realities,* by Milton Erickson, Ernest Rossi, and Sheila Rossi, and *The Collected Papers of Milton H. Erickson on Hypnosis,* vols. I–IV, by Ernest Rossi, Ed.

Glossary

abreaction   Trauma clients may experience intense emotions such as panic or fear which may be accompanied by a flashback or intrusive thought. This expression of emotions may occur during direct treatment of the trauma, but may also occur during simple relaxation. In hypnotherapy, one of several techniques for treating trauma involves age regression to a time the trauma occurred, a facilitated abreaction, and reframing. This process often provides the client with considerable relief and a new understanding of the traumatic experience. This should be attempted only by experienced therapists. Incomplete abreaction of underlying feelings may be a cause of therapeutic failure

absorption of attention   Necessary for successful trance, the client's attention is focused on, for example, a spot on the wall, a story, a bodily sensation, or anything else. Eye fixation, eye closure, facial mask, diminished movement, lack of swallowing, and other signs may indicate an absorption of attention.

age progression   Essentially the opposite of age regression, clients are asked to imagine themselves in the future, feeling or behaving with confidence, strength, or being in control. The technique is also called time projection, among other names.

age regression   A technique useful in hypnotherapy for accessing resources during problem solving and other applications, age regression is experienced naturally whenever someone has a memory or reminiscence. As part of trancework, age regression may be structured and guided (e.g., "I want you to ride a magic carpet back through time to age 15"), or general and permissive (e.g., "I want you, starting now, to go back in your own way, taking as much time as you need, back to any time in the past that might be important to the problem at hand, and when you get there, let me know by nodding your head. . . . "). We should try not to impede clients, as they invariably go back in time much faster than we can guide them.

amnesia   Some practitioners believe that inducing amnesia is necessary for later problem resolution, because amnesia allows unconscious processing to go on without conscious interference. Amnesia can be encouraged with suggestions such as, "Will you forget to remember, or simply remember to forget?" or "When you go to sleep you dream, and when you wake up you cannot remember that dream." Many clients will have amnesia for some portion of the trance experience even if it is not facilitated.

and   A very important word in psychotherapy, *and* leads and links. Following a pacing statement such as, "You feel the comfort of that one deep breath," the word then leads, "*and* you can use that one deep breath to let yourself sink deeper and deeper. . . . " It may also link a truism to a directive or suggestion. For example, "You have experienced the comfort of trance here for the past 30 minutes or so, *and* you can now begin to use this experience at work when you need it the most. . . . "

apposition of opposites An example of hypnotic language, this technique juxtaposes polarities or opposites (e.g., "As that right hand develops a *lightness*, your body can sink even deeper into *heaviness* and relaxation"). The therapist can experiment with warm-cold, up-down, light-heavy, right-left, or any number of opposites.

arm catalepsy Catalepsy means a suspension of movement. An arm catalepsy induction (Gafner & Benson, 2000) involves pacing and leading the subject's cataleptic or rigid arm extended in front of the body. This induction is an effective, rapid, and highly directive means for inducing trance in persons without contraindications, such as cervical pain.

bind of comparable alternatives A potent ally of the therapist, this appears to offer the client a choice between two or more alternatives, offering the illusion of choice (e.g., "Today would you like to go into a light trance, a medium trance, or a deep trance?" or "What you learned today might be useful in your personal life, or maybe you can use it at work, or perhaps you can simply incorporate it into your overall experience").

commitment Social psychology ascertains that if people commit to doing something, they are more likely to comply. A vital concept in hypnotherapy, commitment is a potent therapeutic tool for increasing the effectiveness of suggestions, such as, "Taking one deep breath can help you in a stressful situation. If this is something you're willing to practice at least once a day, your *yes* finger will rise" (see also **unconscious commitment**).

confusion Employed to counter unconscious resistance, this is a broad category of techniques that interrupt, overload, or distract the conscious mind. In this book, confusion is employed in confusional inductions, used for clients who do not respond to more straightforward ones.

conscious—unconscious bind A bind limits choice, channeling behavior in the desired direction. This type of suggestion helps bypass conscious, learned limitations by accessing the unconscious mind (e.g., "An unconscious learning from this experience today may be developed in your conscious mind as well" or "When your conscious mind is ready to provide some useful information about this problem, you will experience a peculiar sensation in your right hand. If such information comes from your unconscious mind, the sensation will be in your left hand").

contingent suggestion   Also known as chaining, this type of suggestion connects the suggestion to an ongoing or inevitable behavior (e.g., "And as you become aware of that peculiar sensation in your right hand, you can begin to float back in time"); or as a posthypnotic suggestion, "When you return here and sit there in that chair, you can resume that deep and pleasant sense of relaxation." It is believed that it is more difficult to reject two or more suggestions when they are linked together in this way.

displacement   As used for pain management, the locus of pain is displaced to another area of the body, or to an area outside the body. The client may continue to experience the sensation, but in a less painful or vulnerable way.

dissociative language   Dissociation is a hallmark of trance and an excellent convincer of trance. The more clients experience it (e.g., their hand separated from their body), the more their hypnotic experience is ratified. Whenever possible, the therapist should say *that* hand instead of *your* hand, and employ similar language, especially during induction and deepening. Encouraging dissociation deepens trance.

double dissociative conscious—unconscious double bind Confusional suggestions such as this are complex and interesting. However, they are probably the least important type of suggestion to become skillful in using. Example: "Between now and next time your conscious mind may work at resolving the problem while your unconscious mind wonders about the implications; or your unconscious mind may come up with answers while your conscious mind ponders the implications."

double negative   An example of hypnotic language, it is believed that a double negative may lead some clients to accept the suggestion more than a simple positive suggestion alone. For example, "You can't not pay attention to the warmth developing in the soles of your feet." The two negatives negate each other to form a positive suggestion, and the hint of confusion enhances acceptance (see also **triple negative**).

embedded suggestion The client's conscious mind is bypassed when the therapist embeds a suggestion. To encourage an inward focus, the therapist may embed *in* words, "Going *in*side can be very *in*teresting . . . *in* there where you have your imag*in*ation, fasc*in*ation, *in*tuition. . . ." Also, the therapist might suggest *security*, for example, by embedding it in a story that emphasizes *security* provided at a large outdoor concert.

eye closure Some therapists feel uncomfortable if clients do not readily close their eyes. We can suggest that their eyes will blink, and their eyelids might feel heavy, and that their eyes can gently close whenever they wish. Clients can experience deep trance through eye fixation alone, and open eyes permit the therapist an observation of ongoing process.

eye fixation For clients who fear loss of control, it is helpful to let them focus their gaze on a spot of their choice, such as somewhere on the wall, the ceiling, or the back of their hand. They may eventually feel comfortable enough to close their eyes.

fluff This refers to meaningless filler that the therapist includes either in the conversational patter in an induction, or in a story. Purposeless, meandering detail is thought to bore the client and deepen absorption. A therapist we work with once said, "It took many years for me to learn to be boring." Too often we may believe that things we say to the client must be purposeful or didactic; however, a few well-placed suggestions inserted amidst a flurry of fluff may be much more effective.

hypnotic language Certain words such as *story, imagine, wonder, curious, explore,* and *interesting* are thought to activate a sense of wonderment, which may enhance the trance process.

implication An important method of indirect suggestion, the therapist stimulates trance experience by conveying positive expectancy. "When you are aware of warmth beginning to spread out, you may nod your head." The therapist does not ask, "*Does* one of your hands feel *light*?" but "*Which* one of your hands is *lighter*?" In implication, *when* is often the operative word, not the authoritarian *will*, which does not imply or suggest, but commands or directs. In accessing unconscious resources, the therapist may say, "Taking as much time as you need, *when* your unconscious mind has selected some strength or resource from the past, your *yes* finger can move all by itself."

interspersal   The therapist's hypnotic patter is interspersed with words, phrases, metaphors, or anecdotes to indirectly influence the client. For example, while therapists count backward from 10 to 1 during deepening, they may insert a brief anecdote about another client who experienced a peculiar heaviness in her hand. Words such as *heavy, light,* or *deep* may be inserted randomly, or a phrase such as "Just let go." Attention is drawn to an interspersed suggestion that is set apart from hypnotic patter by a pause, and thus it becomes more potent.

issues of control and trust   Clients need to be reassured that they will not lose control during the session. Building rapport and trust neutralizes this fear, as does concrete reassurance (e.g., "You are always in the driver's seat") or perhaps humor (e.g., "Don't worry, I'll tell you if you quack like a duck"). Trust is also maintained by discussing the agenda for the session. For example, we would not want to do age regression without permission.

law of parsimony   This "law" holds that the therapist should say or do as little as is necessary to achieve the desired response. A long or elaborate induction is not necessary if the client can go into trance by simply recalling a pleasant scene. With a client experienced in trancework, this less-is-more approach is manifested by a minimalist induction such as "Just sit back now, close your eyes, and let yourself drift off into trance. When you are sufficiently deep, you can let me know by nodding your head."

metaphor   A broad class of indirect techniques, the use of metaphor—understanding one thing by way of another—allows the therapist to bypass the conscious mind and tap into the unconscious process, which tends to be represented and comprehended metaphorically. A client's situation or ideosyncratic speech such as, "I feel like there is a wall around me," provides the therapist with imagery to be utilized. Anecdotes, stories, or symbols stimulate self-referencing at an unconscious level.

naturalistic trance states Prehypnosis discussion should elicit situations when the client naturally drifts off or becomes absorbed in something pleasant, such as a favorite activity. This establishes trance as a naturally occurring behavior within the client's control. Examples include "highway hypnosis" while driving, immersion in a book or a movie.

negative hallucination Milton Erickson employed *positive* hallucination when he had children imagine a furry animal next to them. Even more useful—and easier to induce—is negative hallucination. For example, "You will notice the sound of the air conditioner, people talking in the hallway, and my voice speaking to you, and all these sounds may simply drift in and out of your ears, or you may not hear them at all."

negative reframe To be used judiciously, a negative reframe is useful for redirecting the client's attention or for perturbing monolithic behavior. A man's reluctance to carry out an assignment can be reframed as passivity or weakness. A woman's resentment of her partner can be reframed as uncaring or unprotective.

non sequitur Used for distraction or interruption, a statement that is totally out of context can depotentiate conscious mental sets. One of a wide variety of confusion techniques such as statements or stories, a non sequitur can overload or distract the conscious mind. As the conscious mind seeks to escape from this incongruence or dissonance, the client may be receptive to suggestion, such as an ego strengthening suggestion, "You can do it." Non sequiturs can be virtually any phrase or question, such as, "And the rain fell silently in the forest" or "Do you like dogs?"

not knowing/not doing Actually a suggestion for restraint, this elegant device is very liberating in that it facilitates unconscious responsiveness rather than conscious effort. The therapeutic process may be facilitated if, early in the induction, the therapist says something like, "There's absolutely nothing to do, or to know, or to think about, or to change; in fact, isn't it nice to know that by just sitting there and breathing you can go into trance, and you don't even have to listen to the words." It may also help clients discharge resistance or anxiety.

pattern interruption First noted by Milton Erickson and later explicated by O'Hanlon (Cade & O'Hanlon, 1993), this technique intends to interrupt a symptom by altering one of its component parts, such as frequency, duration, intensity, timing, or location. It is believed that therapists may be more successful disrupting a symptom by altering and thus transforming it, rather than by seeking to totally eliminate it.

permissive suggestion It is believed that many clients respond well when given a wide range of choice. For example, "You may begin to notice sensations, feelings, or experiences beginning to develop in those hands, or will it be in your feet?" The inductions in this book employ a wide variety of suggestions for trance, typically indirectly, allowing the listener to unconsciously self-reference what they choose.

positive expectancy Clients are more likely to be responsive when the therapist conveys confidence and certainty that improvement can be expected. The therapist may express confidence or hopefulness about a successful problem resolution, or during an induction when the therapist suggests hand levitation, both his verbal and nonverbal behavior convey overt positive expectancy.

posthypnotic suggestion This is a suggestion, given in trance, for behavior to occur outside of trance. For example, "When you return here next time and sit down there, the feeling of that chair will be a signal for you to resume the pleasantness and relaxation of trance," or "At work or at home you will be able to begin to relax when you take one big, deep satisfying breath," or "During the next two weeks when you're going to work on the bus and you cross 22nd street, you will *notice something* that can help you with this problem . . . " The last posthypnotic suggestion—notice something—is tagged to a naturally occurring behavior.

prescribing the symptom Employed in paradoxical or strategic therapy, this is a technique that is used to both perturb and counter resistance to change. If, for example, a father excessively criticizes his daughter, he may be asked to continue to criticize her, but "only in the morning between 7:00 and 7:15." Rationales for doing so may be to "study" (for example, "This is interesting and I want you to keep track of it for me") or voluntary control ("This need to criticize seems strong and I'd like you to try and bring it under voluntary control") (see also **pattern interruption**).

pun A play on words, this can cause a sense of wonderment. An embedded suggestion in a pun is a useful indirect technique (e.g., "Your experience in trance today is like an *entrance* into another state" or "You don't need a translator to have a trance later").

question A direct question will focus attention, stimulate associations, and facilitate responsiveness. A question such as "And the tingling down there in that foot, do you notice it yet?" bypasses the conscious mind and is useful as a probe when the therapist is discovering the client's hypnotic talents, or when resistance is present.

reframe A new understanding or appreciation comes about because of new information provided by the therapist. By relabeling or wrapping a positive connotation around problem behavior, the client is given hope and sees the problem in a new light. Virtually anything the client brings to therapy may be reframed. The session itself may be reframed as an effort to make things better. When there is little to reframe, therapists may reframe the presumed motivation *behind* the distress or problem in the same way that they may reframe the therapy session itself as an *effort* or *intention* to make things better. A reframe also sets the stage for a suggestion or directive, so that it is more likely to be accepted. Reframe is a vital element in all methods of psychotherapy, as virtually any behavior can be reframed as strength, protectiveness, caring, or any other value dear to the client (see also **negative reframe**).

repetition Suggestions that are important should be repeated. The therapist may repeat "breathing in comfort and relaxation" several times in an induction. It is also useful to repeat a suggestion in a different way, such as, "feeling a particular heaviness in those feet" may be followed later by the same suggestion that is metaphorical: "Another person felt like he had heavy boots on his feet, and he could barely move them."

resistance A client who says, "I don't want to go into trance" displays conscious resistance. A client who says, "I want to go into trance, but I just can't" is showing unconscious resistance. Many clients are keenly aware of their resistance, which may be anxiety, negativity, or feared loss of control. Resistance may be discharged in various ways including general and permissive suggestions, suggestions covering all possibilities, not knowing/not doing, metaphor, story, confusion techniques, having the client switch chairs (so he leaves his resistance in the first chair), and asking the client questions to which he must answer no (e.g., "In the winter the temperature in Phoenix is the same as Minneapolis"). Many times, clients' resistance will abate as rapport builds, and as they feel more comfortable in therapy.

restraint Resistant clients may become more resistant if we encourage change or adaptation too rapidly. These clients' resistance can be lessened if we restrain or hold them back from moving ahead. For example, "Go slow . . . change presents uncertainty . . . you might not be ready yet . . . it could be dangerous to move ahead too fast." Early in trancework, inducing trance, bringing clients out of trance, and then resuming hypnosis holds back something pleasant, builds responsiveness, and enhances client control.

seeding A suggestion may be more successful when it has been seeded beforehand. A target suggestion is mentioned, or seeded, and later, mentioning the suggestion again, the target is activated. In prehypnosis, the therapist may mention breathing, slowing down, or deep relaxation, as these suggestions will follow in trancework. If therapists know that they will be offering suggestions to slow down eating, they can cue this idea by appreciably slowing down their rhythm in advance.

speaking the client s language By incorporating the client's own language, and literally using the words of the client, the therapist's suggestions may conform more to the client's thinking, and be more effective.

suggestion covering all possibilities This can be especially useful when combined with metaphor. For example, describe someone else's experience in trance: "As a person goes deeper into trance she can begin to notice various sensations starting to develop in her hands. It might be a tingling in one hand; maybe a numbness in the other; perhaps a warm feeling, or a cold one, or some other interesting feeling. One woman one time sitting right there in that chair wondered privately, 'How is it that one time coming in here I can sense a slight coldness up here in my right ear lobe, and another time I feel a tingling down there in my right big toe?'" (see also **bind of comparable alternatives** and **permissive suggestion**).

time distortion This is a common trance phenomenon, as time may seem to speed up or slow down during trance. "How much time do you think has passed since you came in here?" is a relevant question to ask clients when they come out of trance. This ratifies the trance experience and is a measure of responsiveness.

triple negative It is believed that a triple negative is received positively by the unconscious mind. A statement such as "Your unconscious mind *never can't not* process this problem between now and next session" may facilitate processing, or it might best serve to give the client a mild confusion or pleasant sense of wonderment.

truism This is an undeniable statement of fact; for example, "Everyone has felt the warm sun on his or her skin." A series of truisms leads to a yes-set that builds commitment and acceptance of ideas; for example, "Coming in here today on a hot day, sitting for a while out there in the waiting room, walking down the hall, coming in here, and sitting down there, I know that you can begin to let yourself go. . . ." (see also **yes-set**).

unconscious commitment Therapists may consult the unconscious mind through nonverbal signaling, such as, "And when your unconscious mind has identified a time in the past when you felt confident, you may signal with your *yes* finger." Unconscious commitment is obtained by a direct question, such as, "I want to direct a question to your unconscious mind: After exploring this problem and understanding it as you do, are you now willing to let go of the problem? Taking as much time as you need, you may signal with one of your fingers" (see also **commitment**).

unconscious mind Many writers refer to this construct as meaning virtually any thought or feeling that is outside of the client's immediate awareness. With some clients, it may be helpful to refer to this as either "the subsconscious mind" or "the back part of the mind."

utilization Tailoring therapy, or hypnosis, to the individual takes into account the client's unique motivations, interests, preferences, and use of language. The client's behavior, however problematic, is accepted and suggestions are attached to it; for example, the client yawns and the therapist notes, "Have you ever noticed how even a simple yawn can lead to even deeper relaxation?" The therapist conveys the importance of utterly accepting whatever occurs with the client and then seeks to use and transform it. The therapist follows and then guides the ongoing behavior of the client.

yes-set An ally of the therapist in any modality, this involves mentioning truisms, or aspects of undeniable reality, to create a "yes-set" acceptance, thus allowing the client to be more receptive to a suggestion that follows. For example, "You've done very well coming in here for five sessions now, working hard each time, *and* I know that today you can make even more progress toward your goal."

References

Axline, V. (1947). *Play therapy*. New York: Houghton Mifflin.

Barabasz, M., & Spiegel, D. (1989). Hypnotizability and weight loss in obese subjects. *International Journal of Eating Disorders, 8*(3), 335–341.

Bargh, J. A., & Chartrand, T. L. (1999). The unbearable automaticity of being. *American Psychologist, 54*(7), 462–479.

Becker, P. M. (1993). Chronic insomnia: Outcome of hypnotherapeutic intervention in six cases. *American Journal of Clinical Hypnosis, 36*(2), 98–106.

Bellwood, D. R., Hughes, T. P., Folke, C., & Nystrom, M. (2004, June 24). Confronting the coral reef crisis. *Nature, 429*, 827–833.

Bootzin, R. R., Manber, R., Loewy, D. H., Kuo, T. F., & Franzen, P. L (2001). Sleep disorders. In P. B. Sutker & H. E. Adams (Eds.), *Comprehensive handbook of psychopathology* (pp. 671–710). New York: Academic/Plenum.

Cade, B., & O'Hanlon, B. (1993). *A brief guide to brief therapy.* New York: Norton.

Dijksterhuis, A., Bos, M. W., Nordgren, L. F., & Van Baaren, R. B. (2006, February 17). On making the right choice: The deliberation-without-attention effect. *Science, 311*, 1005–1007.

Drake, C. L., Roehers, R., & Roth, R. (2003). Insomnia causes, consequences, and therapeutics: An overview. *Depression and Anxiety, 18*, 163–176.

Edgette, J. H., & Edgette, J. S. (1995). *The handbook of hypnotic phenomena in psychotherapy.* New York: Brunner/Mazel.

Eliot, E. V. (1971). *T. S. Eliot: The complete poems and plays 1909–1950.* New York: Harcourt, Brace, & World.

Erickson, M. H. & Rossi, E. (1981). *Experiencing hypnosis: Therapeutic approaches to altered states.* New York: Irvington.

Felt, B. T., Hall, H., Olness, K., Schmidt, W., Kohen, D., Berman, B. D., Broffman, G., Coury, D., French, G., Dattner, A., & Young, M. H. (1998). Wart regression in children: Comparison of relaxation-imagery to topical treatment and equal time interventions. *American Journal of Clinical Hypnosis, 41*(2), 130–137.

Fletcher, C. (1967). *The man who walked through time.* New York: Random House.

Gafner, G. (2004). *Clinical applications of hypnosis.* New York: Norton.

Gafner, G., & Young, C. (1998). Hypnosis as an adjuvant in the treatment of chronic paranoid schizophrenia. *Contemporary Hypnosis, 15*(4), 223–226.

Gafner, G., & Benson, S. (2000). *Handbook of hypnotic inductions.* New York: Norton.

Gafner, G., Benson, S. (2003). *Hypnotic techniques.* New York: Norton.

Geary, B. (1994). Seeding responsiveness to hypnotic processes. In J. Zeig (Ed.), *Ericksonian methods: The essence of the story* (pp. 315–332). New York: Brunner/Mazel.

Gibbons, D. E. (1979). *Applied hypnosis and hyperempiria.* New York: Plenum.

Gonsalkorale, W. M., Houghton, L. A., & Whorwell, P. J. (2002). Hypnotherapy in irritable bowel syndrome: A large-scale audit of a clinical service with examination of factors influencing responsiveness. *American Journal of Gastroenterology, 97*(4), 954–961.

Green, J., Barabasz, A., Barrett, D., & Montgomery, G. (2005). The 2003 APA division 30 definition of hypnosis. *American Journal of Clinical Hypnosis, 48,* 2–3, 89.

Hammond, D. C. (1990). *Handboook of hypnotic suggestions and metaphors.* New York: Norton.

Harvey, A. G., & Payne, S. (2002). The management of unwanted pre-sleep thoughts in insomnia: Distraction with imagery versus general distraction. *Behaviour Research and Therapy, 40,* 267–277.

Haynes, S. N., Adams, A., & Franzen, M. (1981). The effect of presleep stress on sleep-onset insomnia. *Journal of Abnormal Psychology, 90,* 601–606.

Helgason, C. (2006). Unpublished manuscript.

Houghton, L. A., Heyamn, D. J., & Whorwell, P. J. (1996). Symptomatology, quality of life, and economic features of irritable bowel syndrome: The effect of hypnotherapy. *Alimentary Pharmacology and Therapeutics, 10,* 91–95.

Jacobs, I. (2005). Unpublished manuscript.

Jacobs, E., Pelier, E., & Larkin, D. (1998). Ericksonian hypnosis and approaches with pediatric hematology oncology patients. *American Journal of Clinical Hypnosis, 41*(2), 139–154.

Kroger, W. S. (1963). *Clinical and experimental hypnosis in medicine, dentistry, and psychology*. Philadelphia: Lippincott.

Lambe, R., Osier, C., & Franks, P. (1986). A randomized controlled trial of hypnotherapy for smoking cessation. *The Journal of Family Practice, 22*(1), 61–65.

Lovinger, S. L. (1998). *Child psychotherapy*. Northvale, NJ: Jason Aronson.

Mills, J. C., & Crowley, R. J. (1986). *Therapeutic metaphors for children and the child within*. New York: Brunner/Mazel.

Ohayon, M. M. (2002). Epidemiology of insomnia: What we know and what we still need to learn. *Sleep Medicine Review, 6*(2), 97–11.

Olness, K., & Cohen, D. P. (1996). *Hypnosis and hypnotherapy with children*. New York: Guilford.

Papp, P. (1983). *The process of change*. New York: Guilford.

Salkovskis, P. M., & Campbell, P. (1994). Thought suppression induces intrusion in naturally occurring negative intrusive thoughts. *Behaviour Research and Therapy, 32*, 1–8.

Shaffer, D. H. (1980). *Clocks: The Smithsonian illustrated library of antiques*. Washington, DC: Smithsonian Institution.

Spanos, N. P., Williams, V., & Gwynn, M. I. (1990). Effects of hypnotic, placebo, and salicylic acid treatments on wart regression. *Psychosomatic Medicine, 52*(1), 109–114.

Stanton, H. E. (1985). Permissive vs. authoritarian approaches in clinical and experimental settings. In J. K. Zeig (Ed.), *Ericksonian psychotherapy, vol. I: Structures* (pp. 293–304). New York: Brunner/Mazel.

Steele, S. B. (1996). Mr. Holt's horse. In B. Patton (Ed.), *Tales from the Canadian Rockies* (pp. 110–111). Toronto, Canada: McClelland & Stewart. (Original work published 1883.)

Stratton, E. K. (1997). *Seeds of light*. New York: Simon & Schuster.

Wallas, L. (1985). *Stories for the third ear*. New York: Norton.

Winerman, L. (2006). From the stage to the lab. *Monitor on Psychology*, *37*(3), 26–27.

Yapko, M. D. (2005–2006), Some comments regarding the division 30 definition of hypnosis. *American Journal of Clinical Hypnosis*, *48*(2–3), 107–110.

Zahourek, R. P. (1985). *Clinical hypnosis and therapeutic suggestion in nursing*. New York: Grune & Stratton.

Zeig, J. K. (1985). The clinical use of amnesia: Ericksonian methods. In J. K. Zeig (Ed.), *Ericksonian psychotherapy: vol. 1: Structures* (pp. 317–337). New York: Brunner/Mazel.

Index